Philosophy
after Friendship

Philosophy *after* Friendship

Deleuze's Conceptual Personae

GREGG LAMBERT

UNIVERSITY OF MINNESOTA PRESS

MINNEAPOLIS • LONDON

An earlier version of chapter 1 was published as "Deleuze and the Political Ontology of 'the Friend' (philos)," in *Deleuze and Politics*, ed. Ian Buchanan and Nick Thoburn, 35–53 (Edinburgh: Edinburgh University Press, 2008). An earlier version of chapter 2 was published as "Enemy *(der Feind),*" *Angelaki: Theoretical Journal of the Humanities* 12, no. 3 (2007); reprinted by permission of the publisher Taylor & Francis, http://tandfonline.com. An earlier version of chapter 3 was published as "Universal Hospitality," in *Cities without Citizens,* ed. Aaron Levy and Eduardo Cadava, 13–32 (Philadelphia: Slought Books, 2003). An earlier version of chapter 6 was published as "The War-Machine and 'A People Who Revolt,'" *Theory & Event* 13, no. 3 (2010).

Published by the University of Minnesota Press
111 Third Avenue South, Suite 290
Minneapolis, MN 55401-2520
http://www.upress.umn.edu

Printed in the United States of America on acid-free paper

The University of Minnesota is an equal-opportunity educator and employer.

22 21 20 19 18 17   10 9 8 7 6 5 4 3 2 1

Library of Congress Cataloging-in-Publication Data
Names: Lambert, Gregg, author.
Title: Philosophy after friendship : Deleuze's conceptual personae / Gregg Lambert.
Description: Minneapolis : University of Minnesota Press, [2017] | Includes bibliographical
    references and index.
Identifiers: LCCN 2016015349| ISBN 978-1-5179-0099-1 (hc) | ISBN 978-1-5179-0100-4 (pb)
Subjects: LCSH: Deleuze, Gilles, 1925–1995. | Friendship—Philosophy. | Philosophy, Modern—
    20th century.
Classification: LCC B2430.D454 L353 2017 | DDC 194—dc23
LC record available at https://lccn.loc.gov/2016015349

As to the utility of such an universal and lasting peace, supposing a plan for that purpose practicable, and likely to be adopted, there can be but one voice. The objection, and the only objection to it, is the apparent impracticability of it—that it is not only hopeless, but that to such a degree that any proposal to that effect deserves the name of visionary and ridiculous. This objection I shall endeavor in the first place to remove; for the removal of this prejudice may be necessary to procure for the plan a hearing.

What can be better suited to the preparing of men's minds for the reception of such a proposal than the proposal itself?

Let it not be objected that the age is not ripe for such a proposal: the more it wants of being ripe, the sooner we should begin to do what can be done to ripen it; the more we should do to ripen it. A proposal of this sort, is one of those things that can never come too early nor too late.

—JEREMY BENTHAM, "A Plan for an Universal and Perpetual Peace" (1843)

Contents

~~Philos~~ophy after Friendship

*Prolegomena for a
"Post-War" Philosophy*

> We are no longer Greeks and Friendship is no longer the same.
>
> —GILLES DELEUZE AND FÉLIX GUATTARI, *What Is Philosophy?*

Late in his life, immediately following the publication *of Foucault* (1986) and prior to the publication of *What Is Philosophy?* (1991), Gilles Deleuze engaged in a brief exchange of letters with Dionys Mascolo, the author of *Le Communisme* (1953) and *Autour d'un effort de mémoire: Sur une lettre de Robert Antelme* (1988). This correspondence, which is to form the fulcrum of this study, concerns the writings of both Mascolo and Maurice Blanchot on the theme of friendship *(amitié).* In his correspondence, Deleuze speaks (very obliquely) of certain "concrete situations" that have caused the concept of *phílos* to become displaced from its original Greek sources of *phileîn* and *philía,* a displacement that he says has undergone through the war an experience that can be likened to aphasia and amnesia and that he and Félix Guattari claim less than five years later requires nothing less than a "complete re-evaluation of philosophy."[1]

Taking these comments to heart, in the following reflections I attempt to reconstruct a genealogy of the different concrete situations and social personae to which this final statement might refer in order to arrive at

1

a moment of recollection where perhaps the essential meaning of philosophy might be interrogated anew, especially in relation to Deleuze's assertion that the democratic ideal of friendship has become corrupted to the point, today, where it may be completely "rotten" *(pourri)*.[2] Consequently, following the revelation that I first encountered in the correspondence between Deleuze and Mascolo around the concept of "the friend" *(phílos)*—a conversation that returns a few years later with Guattari in the opening of *What Is Philosophy?*—I propose to bracket, or, according to the Heideggerian gesture, *to cross out in order to completely work through (durcharbeiten),* a very commonplace and patently metaphorical equivalence between the ideas of friendship and the democratic form of politics. In other words, by crossing out the original Greek concept of *phílos* in the above title, I am only attempting to suspend some of the traditional associations that have overdetermined our understanding of the political sphere as a higher realm of friendship, which today can only have a metaphorical equivalent (which might be based on nothing more than an "etymological fallacy" that is derived from the poetic resources of the Greek language). In fact, the term "friend" actually refers to an original and even primitive "conceptual persona" first invented by the Greeks, the meaning of which is now difficult to discern, as we will see, since many of its social and ritual significations have become hopelessly and perhaps irretrievably lost. Nevertheless, concerning the friend *(phílos)* and the related concepts of the stranger *(perigrinus,* the stranger-wanderer or foreigner, and *xénos,* the stranger-guest), I attempt to recover a few aspects of their original social significations.

In many respects, my research of these concepts and their corresponding conceptual personae has been greatly influenced by the etymological analysis of the famous Indo-European linguist Émile Benveniste, whose two-volume *Le Vocabulaire des institutions Indo-Européennes* has come to represent for me a touchstone of sorts; although, certainly my main source of inspiration can be found in a description from the first chapter of *What Is Philosophy?* that "every concept has a history, even though this history zig-zags . . . through other problems or onto different planes."[3]

In fact, this perfectly describes the organization of this book and represents my own attempt to reconstruct an etymological history of the concept of "the friend" by constructing a genealogy that passes through the various problems posed by the concepts of the enemy and the stranger, concepts that have bifurcated and occupy entirely different planes composed by the Greek (or Hellenic), Roman, Christian, and finally, the modern, secularized world. As the reader will note, I have rendered the term of each conceptual persona in different languages (ancient Greek, Latin, German, and French) in an effort to historicize the genealogy I am attempting to reconstruct, perhaps by giving it more of an epic form rather than that of a simple vocabulary or glossary of terms. In short, this is my own experimental method of addressing Deleuze's description of etymology as "a specifically philosophical athleticism," since in my reconstruction of this genealogy—while some concepts call for archaisms (e.g., *perigrinus, xénos*) and others for more modern terms (e.g., *der Feind*)—all these concepts as well as their conceptual personae are "shot through with almost crazy etymological exercises."[4]

For example, returning to the common misconception that would place the concepts of friend and stranger in opposition to each other (although in a manner that is different from the friend–enemy grouping), as Benveniste shows, the original term actually belongs to the ancient institution of hospitality *(xénia)* and designates the ritual persona of the "stranger-guest" *(hôte)*. Of course, this primitive sense of obligation has evolved in modern societies to acquire different moral, ethical, juridical, and legal senses that have overdetermined its social meaning, often coloring the social relationship with mysterious affective or sentimental determination that Benveniste argues did not actually belong to the original meaning of *phileîn* and *philía* (friendship). What is even more surprising than the discovery of a uniquely sentimental determination of "friend" that "at first, does not imply any truly social notions" (e.g., duty, obligation, hospitality, etc.) is the conclusion that this association can be originally found in only one language (i.e., Greek).[5] This immediately leads to Benveniste's remarkable conclusion that it is the Greek language itself that is responsible for these later sentimental and affective qualities that now overdetermine the conceptual persona of "the friend," and this occurred in a manner that he compares to dream-work.[6] As I discuss in greater detail below, certainly Benveniste was aware that this argument would appear counterintuitive to the widespread and commonplace sentimental associations of the terms "friendship" and "friend," and his evocation of the Freudian process of the dream-work stands for an interpretation of this "proto-historical" process of displacement or condensation of earlier traces of memory and experience that belong to language and culture.

In my own study, I could not pursue this etymological history through all its ramifications, especially concerning how a historical language might actually dream and how this dream would have real historical and cultural effects in the translation of this language's concepts and terms into other languages (such as Latin, German, and French), *each of which may also have its own specific manner of dreaming*. Instead, I have simply highlighted this metaphorical and poetic overdetermination of the Homeric concept on the authority of Benveniste's etymological analysis in an effort to recover some of the concept's original social meaning. Although the concept of hospitality has been a commonplace topic in contemporary philosophy, especially following the writings of Jacques Derrida (who is also directly influenced by Benveniste's etymological analyses of Indo-European institutions), my own study focuses almost exclusively on the conceptual persona of the "stranger-guest," which also bears a secondary meaning of "stranger-friend," a particular kind of friendship that can only exist between a host and various types of strangers, or foreigners *(perigrini, advenae)*, but, as we will see, especially those strangers "who have been deprived of all political rights" (although this same relation could evolve into the enemy opposition as well, as demonstrated by the contemporary polarity that defines the original Greek term *xénos)*.[7]

Nevertheless, returning to the insight that the relation of friendship might originally bear no affective traits of sentimentality or emotion that are now attached to the social relationship today, this might allow us to understand the origin of a relationship of dependency and mutual

obligation, which becomes the condition of any ethical or juridical relationship to strangers, as well as the basis for international law and the
treatment of the rights of strangers beginning in the eighteenth century,
which also marks the appearance of Immanuel Kant's treatise *Zum ewi-
gen Frieden* (1795), where we find the important appendix on "Universal Hospitality."[8] In fact, simply as an exercise, I might even suggest that
we restrict the usage of the term "friend" only to the social relation
with certain strangers and particularly to "those strangers that have
been deprived of all political rights." I realize that this may simply be
the substitution of one metaphor for another (i.e., of an archaic for a
modern one), and thus I could easily be accused of committing another
"etymological fallacy." In response, I might suggest that such a "crazy
etymological exercise" could also approximate the process of the original dream-work mentioned above—that is, as a corrective to the
condensation and displacement of historical and cultural significations
that have overdetermined the concept of friendship and the conceptual
persona of the friend over several centuries of Occidental thought.

In the opening pages of their last work, Deleuze and Guattari also return to take up a distinctly modern concept of "the friend" *(l'ami)* in
order to highlight our own historical and existential distance from the
distinctively Greek idea of friendship that appeared as one of the primary
subjective virtues of the early city-state, which was fashioned to contain
the intensive states of competition, rivalry, and civil conflict *(stásis)*
between citizens in the form of a "generalized athleticism" where the
primary virtue of friendship would also be judged in ethical and aesthetic terms. In this sense, the idea of friendship would also lead directly
to the consensus of the common, moral notions of the good, aesthetic
judgments of beauty and ugliness, and the creation of a distinctive form
of politi-cal "opinion" that belonged to the Greek "assembly" *(ekklesia,*
later on meaning "church" in the Christian era), where the number of
actual citizens who could legitimately be called "friends" was less than
one thousand in any given polis—that is, constituting a group of citizens
that was smaller than the population of an average village in the same

territory. Simply accounting for the difference in scale in comparison with modern societies, is it any wonder that the original concrete situation of friendship has become too abstract, given the increasing diversity of the relationships that define urban and cosmopolitan centers in the modern world?

Today we might ask whether polities (from the Greek term *politika*), which was used to designate a privileged place *(topos)* for the display of civil conflict *(stásis),* can any longer contain the extreme states of conflict that constantly break out in modern societies—conflicts initially between races, classes, and nations that, in the contemporary world, have evolved even further into the extreme opposition between richest and poorest populations that belong to the global polis.[9] As Hannah Arendt first asked following the emergence of totalitarianism, can the contemporary democratic ideal of universal rights *(consensus iuris),* which Cicero first defined as the consensual definition of right that is the basis for the entity of a "people," be actually understood as the consensus of equals and respect for the dignity of human rights?[10] Or rather, in the absolute newness of totalitarian law itself, which represented a conscious break with any principle of consensus with the peoples of the earth, does the name of "politics" today only designate a fragile alliance that pretends to hold together the various national interests in a lawful accord but in almost all other areas of civil society seeks to preserve the independence of each species-being in its incessant striving for its own biopolitical life? According to Arendt's earliest and most prescient intuition, which already prefigures Michel Foucault's later thesis of "biopower," what is historically unprecedented in totalitarian policy is its claim to "transform the human species into an active unfailing carrier of a law to which human beings otherwise would only passively and reluctantly be subjected."[11] From this point onward, the rationalizing principle of power expands from its earlier juridical forms of sovereignty to become indistinguishable from the laws that govern evolutionary biology and the immunology of living organisms; thus, as a result of this change in principle, *man becomes a "carrier of the law," rather than its subject.* According to a well-known statement by Friedrich Hayek, "The individual cannot activate its species-being [its biopolitical value] by participating in the *polis*."[12] The concentration of biological and economic life and the consequent reduction of the political sphere is fundamental to Giorgio Agamben's critical appropriation of the concept of biopower, as well as to most current interpretations of neoliberal society. However, if the consensual spirit of law is abandoned altogether, either in favor of the laws of "movement and history," as Arendt earlier argued in the case of totalitarian polity, or in the favor of purely economic law, as has been argued today concerning the polity of neoliberal "governmentality" (Foucault), then there can no longer be a principle of politics between "peoples," strictly speaking, only a kind of "generalized Machiavellianism" (Mascolo).[13]

Returning now to Deleuze's earlier statement, if every original virtue has been so permeated by money today, to the point where every form of interest is either corrupted—if not altogether "rotten" *(pourri)*—then what happens in this new situation to the concept of *phílos* itself, which originated in Occidental thought from the earlier period of the Greeks onward and already prefigures the intersubjective idealism of politics in late-democratic societies? And further then, what of Communism? Has it not also been called, in many of its more utopian versions, a "universal society of friendship"? It is precisely to these questions that Deleuze returns in an interview with Italian Marxist Antonio Negri in the spring of 1990, where Negri raises the question of friendship in the age of the universals of communication and marketing, to ask whether it still constitutes a utopian version of politics today. He asks:

> In the Marxist utopia of the *Grundrisse*, communism takes precisely the form of a transversal organization of free individuals built on technology that makes it possible. Is communism still a viable option? Maybe in a communication society it's less utopian than it used to be?[14]

Thus, in the conclusion to *What Is Philosophy?* Deleuze and Guattari proclaim the idea of the universal market as perhaps the greatest threat to a philosophical notion of friendship, since neoliberal ideology has converted the original athleticism of the Greek concept of *stásis* into pure economic competition between so-called equals, and the lively debates of opinion over the philosophical questions of the beautiful and "the good life" have become the new universals of communication and marketing but in a manner that no longer corresponds to the political as such, but rather to a kind of permanent and generalized Machiavellianism mediated only by an open—although not necessarily public—sphere of commerce and private finance.[15]

It is not by accident that in 1991, within a year of these earlier correspondences with Mascolo and Negri, Deleuze and Guattari argue that the original concept of philosophy has been placed "under so much distress" that the early philosophical analogy to the social experience of friendship may no longer designate a "living category" from which contemporary forms of political association can be thought. As they write:

> The question is important because the friend who appears in philosophy no longer stands for an extrinsic persona, an example or empirical circumstance, but rather for a presence that is intrinsic to thought, a condition of possibility of thought itself, a living category, *a transcendental lived reality [un veçu transcendental]*.[16]

In other words, confronted by the perceived loss of its original ground, either through the ideological corruption of the concept itself or by centuries of violence and warfare, the philosophical idea of friendship as an image of thought peacefully divided within/between two beings who think this division in common, in their final work Deleuze and Guattari return to reflect on the question of whether what they thought they had been doing together all along could any longer be called "philosophy." "It had to be possible," they write, "to ask the question 'between friends' as a secret or a confidence, or even as a challenge when confronting the enemy, and at the same time to reach that twilight hour when one distrusts even the friend."[17]

In the above passage we also find a cryptic reference to the figure of Friedrich Hölderlin, who is also the frequent subject of Martin Heidegger's mediations on "the autochthonic [Greek] friend" and who is also alluded to earlier on in Deleuze's correspondence with Mascolo as "the German poet who wrote in the twilight hour." Of course, given the significance of this "German poet" in Heidegger's own reflections on the original relation between *phileîn* and *philía,* here we might understand that the friend whom one should be wary of is Heidegger himself, who should be distrusted for obvious reasons, *particularly any political destination of philosophy after Heidegger's fundamental betrayal of precisely this relationship.*[18] It is perhaps for this reason, moreover, that the history of contemporary philosophy has increasingly been marked by new revelations of the same betrayal, each one more damning than the last, followed by a series of mitigations that seek to save the name of philosophy from its own catastrophe. In addition to Derrida's commentary, we find perhaps the most sober assessment of this episode in the following passage from *What Is Philosophy?*

> The Heidegger affair has complicated matters: a great philosopher had to be reterritorialized on Nazism for the strangest commentaries to meet up, sometimes calling his philosophy into question, and sometimes absolving it through such complicated and convoluted arguments that we are still in the dark. . . . How could Heidegger's concepts not be intrinsically sullied by an abject reterritorialization? Unless all concepts include this grey zone and indiscernibility, where for a moment the combatants on the ground are confused, and the thinker's eye mistakes one for the other—not only the German for a Greek but a fascist for a creator of existence and freedom.[19]

It is on the basis of this "concrete situation" that the relationship between philosophy and politics must be situated in light of the above comment, since it is precisely on the original ground where philosophy was first defined on the basis of the social relation of friendship, as "a conversation between friends" *(philótēs),* that a new situation has emerged where this earlier ground itself is overcome by confusion and the mistaken identity of the original interlocutors (friend, enemy, and stranger), thus causing the conversation to undergo an essential experience of aphasia and stammering.[20]

As a result of this catastrophe we must ask, by what authority does philosophy continue speaking of human rights today? That is to say, if philosophy is no longer Greek, as Deleuze and Guattari say, then this also implies that the autochthonic conceptual persona of the "celestial stranger" (who appears at the center of the polis, having descended from the sky, or arriving from everywhere) has changed sense and appearance (i.e., "faciality"), meaning the concrete social relation to a particular class of strangers that functions to animate the mask that the modern philosopher wears, a mask that is fashioned from the different classes of actual strangers that populate the modern world. As Deleuze and Guattari write, the irony of the Hellenic autochthony was already that, while it conditioned the emergence of the *Imperium* in relation to the city-states as the prefiguration of the modern nations, this milieu is only realized inasmuch as it establishes conjunctions with strangers, aliens, and immigrants who come from afar. As they write, "These types come from the borderland of the Greek world, strangers in flight, breaking with the empire and colonized by the peoples of Apollo—not only artisans and merchants but also philosophers."[21] In the modern period (and, I argue, in "post-war" philosophy especially), we have witnessed an entirely new class of "strangers in flight" and, thus, a different series of masks and distinctly new conceptual personae who today have emerged to say "I"—that is, strangers, refugees, deportees, subhumans, and so on. As a result, the philosopher's vision of the polis or the political is no longer the survey of a central point that radiates outward until it is reterritorialized onto every part of the earth but instead is often established *from the perspective of a periphery,* even from an archipelago of invisible or unconscious zones, including ghettos, camps, and shanty-towns that are absent from any official *census.* In other words, beginning at some point—again, we might say, at least since "the war"—philosophy begins to *orient* its thinking and critique of the political through this new series of conceptual personae, each of which in turn is directly linked to a certain territory, or zone, as well as to a distinctive new class of strangers through which the philosopher speaks in order to critique the limits of the political. For example, when Hannah Arendt writes "we refugees"—who, moreover, prefer to be called "newcomers" or "immigrants"—she is addressing not only the status of a dominant representation of a new class of strangers in American society but the philosophical features of a new conceptual persona in modern political philosophy.

At this point we must turn to another distinction that Deleuze and Guattari make immediately after discussing the difference between aesthetic figures and conceptual personae, which is the distinction between what they call psychosocial types. This returns us to perhaps the first definition of the conceptual personage as a being that appears within the *socius* and whose origin (or historical selection) remains somewhat mysterious. This distinction is important because these figures appear natural in their territories, and it turns out that we are living among these persona constantly, if not embodied by them. In fact, these can be called deterritorialized personae, most of which were once conceptual personae invented by philosophy itself but whose functions have changed sense and now belong to another system or unconscious structure (i.e., "like a language"). The examples of these personae or psychosocial types include the friend (apart from its original Greek situation) as well as the stranger, the nomad, the exile, the transient, the migrant, and the foreigner; to these we could also add the types of the enemy or the barbarian. To identify these psychosocial types as "deterritorialized conceptual personae" means that they no longer express a relation to immanence of a vital concept but rather a connection to a "category of common characteristics" (from *tupos*, also meaning impression, figure, or face, and including the facial features that make up social stereotypes).

Deleuze and Guattari refer to these types as "mobile territories" in the sense that the subject can leave home or his native land and carry all these types with him in order to populate another territory or even a universe with these psychosocial types. For example, the stranger will mark a particular psychosocial type, created from law and culture, that can be found everywhere and thus establish a relation and an orientation toward the home or to the native land and, at the same time, toward the hinterland, the frontier, the outback, or even the strange and mysterious land populated by fabulous creatures ("oh what a brave new world, and such marvelous creatures in it"). This is why Deleuze and Guattari always situate the existence of psychosocial types or personages in direct relation to the concept of territory and locate the creation of new personages in the movements of territorialization and deterritorialization. This becomes important for the Greek concept of polis and the autochthonic personage of the stranger through the history of its own deterritorialization throughout the Mediterranean world. In the early Christian world, the stranger and the immigrant (*ethnē*) become distinctive psychosocial types for the "mobile territories" of Jews and Christians across Asia Minor that end up in Rome as the basis for the creation of a new people and a new earth; later, they undergo a statutory and legal transformation through the deterritorialization that is effected by European colonialism and, today, the deterritorialization of "the West" through the process of globalization. It is true that this movement at each stage already grasps the stranger as a living psychosocial type even though it remains an abstraction until it is embodied or territorialized on a particular class or ethnic group, but this movement is also territorialized on the subject who is endowed with rights, secured by an equally autochthonic claim to territory and soil, to nation and language, which first endows the right to function as a host, including the power to name and to assign the type (for example, to institute the stranger–guest relationship). At the same time, Deleuze and Guattari differentiate these psychosocial types from conceptual personae since in many ways their identity is that of former conceptual personae that have been lost or forgotten in their concepts and become clichés of actual living social relations. Consequently, they write:

> We cannot even say what comes first, and perhaps every territory presupposes a prior deterritorialization, or everything happens at the same time. Social fields are inextricable knots in which the three movements

are mixed up so that, in order to disentangle them, we have to *diagnose real types or personae.*[22]

This seems to be a crucial passage, and in part it will provide the method for this study, in the sense that it outlines a properly diagnostic and genealogical task that takes up these psychosocial types that inhabit us (and we inhabit) in order to restore them to the function of conceptual personae. Of course, this does not imply that it is possible to return to the original conceptual personae from which these types first derived— for example, to restore the original Greek concept of *phílos*—as if to restore the psychosocial type to its autochthonic territory of homeland, as in the case of Heidegger's conceptual persona of the philosopher and the poet. Therefore, a "diagnostic" treatment of these types means placing them in relation to the immanence of the concept again, *revealing them in relation to their own proper territories* by producing a genealogical account that frees these conceptual personae from their archaic psychosocial types—that is to say, from archaic territories that are deterritorialized in our own heads and, at the same time, reterritorialized onto the earth.

Drawing once again on the definition of the social stranger from Benveniste, which will be crucial in our understanding of the original link between the philosophical enunciation of conceptual personae and what Deleuze and Guattari call psychosocial types:

> The stranger is "one who comes from outside" (Lat. *aduena*), or simply, one who is beyond the limits of community (Lat. *perigrinus*). . . . Consequently, *there is no "stranger" as such* . . . [since] the stranger is always a *particular* stranger, as one who originates from a distinct statute.[23]

In Benveniste's definition we find the vital manner by which the original conceptual persona of the philosopher, in its identification with a "particular class of strangers" that occupied the Hellenic world, has evolved throughout history, also recalling Deleuze and Guattari's observation that philosophy has always identified with a nomadic band of those who come from outside, or who appear from beyond the limits of community. (In fact, it is from the composite features of this original grouping that populated the Hellenic world that the autochthonic mask of the "celestial stranger" was born.) At the same time, we must also observe from the above definition that *"there is no stranger as such,"* and therefore in each case the features that animate the philosopher's mask are strictly empirical in origin, since these features and various facial types arrive through a distinct statute (or positive law) that determines particular social strangers, given that for every age, and for every territory, "the stranger is always a *particular* stranger."

Most recently, of course, the figure of *homo sacer* comes immediately to mind as a vivid demonstration of both the above observations. Thus, Agamben derives his unique conceptual persona from two distinctive statuses or codices, one archaic and one modern in origin: first, from a codicil on Roman sacrificial law by Pompeius Festus where, according to Agamben's claims, "the character of sacredness is tied for the first time to human life as such"; second, of course, from the laws passed in Germany in 1933, a few weeks after Hitler's rise to power, that protected the hereditary purity of the German people and thus functioned as a legal precedent for the racial laws against the Jewish populations under the Third Reich.[24] Nevertheless, it is the leap between these two statutes or codices that directly links them together—at once archaic and modern, Roman and German, Christian and Jewish—and that refers to Agamben's unique conceptual creation, which has effectively modernized the political concept of the stranger and has made *homo sacer* a dramatic vehicle for contemporary political and philosophical enunciation.

On the one hand, we can only admire the dramaturgy introduced by the creation of this new conceptual persona, a dramaturgy that continues to orient the thinking of the concept of the political in the current moment, and particularly in the post 9/11 context, where the refugee, the deportee, and the enemy have continued to evolve by a new set of determinations stemming from positive laws (such as the Patriot Act). Although we might immediately wish to acknowledge how these figures appear differently than in the earlier writings of Primo Levi or Hannah Arendt from which they are drawn, they belong to the same constellation of types and the new conceptual personae that have marked the extreme "limit-situations" of our political modernity. On the other hand, we might also fault the concept on several levels: first, for its strange admixture of political theology and positive law (i.e., the amalgamation of Walter Benjamin and Carl Schmitt, the quintessential Jewish thinker and infamous Nazi jurist); second, following Derrida's own criticisms in the late seminar on the figures of sovereignty, for the manner of re-territorializing the concept onto the original ground from which Greek philosophy first emerged since Aristotle. Recalling the earlier comment by Deleuze and Guattari, can we not say that Agamben's specific reterritorialization has only served to complicate matters even further—albeit, certainly in a manner that is completely different from Heidegger's re-territorialization on Greece, even though they are not entirely unrelated—and that on this same ground we discover there is still a great deal of confusion and mistaken identity between both ancient and modern combatants, not only between "who is the friend?" and "who is the enemy?" but also, today, between Greek and Roman, German and Jew, and American and Muslim?

For the purposes of my own study of these figures, rather than drawing on Agamben's conceptual persona of *homo sacer* I have chosen instead an episode that is important for both Deleuze and Blanchot, concerning the earlier figure of Robert Antelme, who becomes a central figure regarding reflection on the conceptual personae of the friend, the deportee, and the survivor.[25] It is around the concrete situation that I have already evoked above as an experience of amnesia and aphasia that we will first find an explicit reference to Antelme: a leader of the French Resistance and the friend of Mascolo himself, who returns from Dachau (rescued by Mascolo, a young François Mitterand, and also by his former spouse, Marguerite Duras), and whose gradual recovery from a state of the broken and completely exhausted victim of the camp, "the bag of tattered rags and bones," is later recounted in detail by Duras in her memoire, *La Douleur* (1985). It is from these early days of recovery, and in a barely discernible voice, that Antelme converses with a company of friends who have gathered around him and gives testimony to the catastrophic violence he had experienced, which later becomes the testament contained in the pages of *L'Éspece humane* (1947). From this experience is born the figure of Antelme in our genealogy of the conceptual persona of "the friend," which becomes extremely significant for both Mascolo and Blanchot, who, in their own respective efforts to remember the experience that Antelme converts into the living relation of friendship, must acknowledge the very impossibility of an experience that remains both "in-common" *(Mitsein)* and yet "un-sharable." In his own commentary on the new conceptual persona of the philosopher as "a Socrates who becomes Jewish," Deleuze explicitly invokes the writings of Blanchot but also the importance of Mascolo's idea of communism as the "absolute spirit of friendship," even though we must now understand the concept of "the friend" as stemming from the concrete experience of catastrophe and existing after it.[26] Thus, in his letter to Mascolo, Deleuze himself refers to Antelme's experience as our new "limit-situation," thus providing the image of a new conceptual persona of a friend who exists in the wake of a catastrophe, having encountered "the extreme limit of pain" (echoing an image of Hölderlin's earlier episode of madness and aphasia in France).[27]

Of course, I realize that by invoking the figure of Antelme, the deportee and survivor of the camp, my own discourse risks becoming somewhat anachronistic today in light of an incredible effort, it seems, to stop invoking the camp as a paradigm of our political modernity *á la Agamben*—that is, to move beyond a thanatopolitical framework in order to discover a more positive (or "affirmative") biopolitical order, as expressed in the recent works of Roberto Esposito, Rosi Braidotti, and many others (including Agamben himself!).[28] Despite my suspicions that this move is purely *speculative* (also in a marketing sense of the term), it may also risk vacating an important frame of reference before completely understanding how the experience of a survivor (and not simply the "victim" of the camp or gulag) might foretell something concerning our own "biopolitical futures."[29] In order to avoid any association of Antelme's persona with Agamben's figure of *homo sacer,* however, I would simply point out that while the latter is a pure figure stripped of all human resemblance, especially speech, and thus reduced to a "paradigm" of bare life, by contrast, as Duras recounts in her memoir, Antelme actually insists on speaking in an incredible effort to maintain the memory of what happened, even when his friends tell him that "by itself his physical appearance was eloquent enough." Finally, my representation of the figure of Antelme as a conceptual persona of the deportee and survivor is made without the least hint of dramaturgy (as in the case of Agamben), much less the narrative basis of a new martyriology or hagiography (although there will be features of these quasi-religious genres in both Blanchot's and Mascolo's written accounts), but rather serves only as a philosophical allegory of the possible survival of the concept of friendship itself after an ordeal that has evacuated its previous meanings, since in order to survive and undergo the possibility of renewal in the so-called post-war period, which I will return to question below, the idea of friendship itself may also need to pass through something that at least resembles the experiences of amnesia and aphasia.

"Unless we are led back to 'the Friend,'" as Deleuze and Guattari write:

> but after an ordeal that is too powerful, an inexpressible catastrophe, so yet another new sense, in a mutual distress, a mutual weariness that forms the new right of thought *(Socrates becomes Jewish)*. Not two friends who communicate and recall the past together but, on the contrary, who both suffer an amnesia or aphasia capable of splitting thought, of dividing it in itself.[30]

In other words, certainly, today one can say that "we are no longer Greeks and friendship is no longer the same."[31] The idea of friendship certainly has suffered from an essential amnesia or aphasia and no longer signifies thought being divided within itself according to the categories of unity and equality, either because the living category of the friend no longer signifies this identity of thought thinking itself or because friendship has exhausted this division, originated by the Greeks, and we must conclude that the historical image of friendship may no longer have anything in common with philosophy from the present moment onward. In other words, philosophy can no longer refer to a living category to ground its own concept of the political, and its historical image of thought can no longer encompass the living social dialectic without leading it into a violent contradiction, which in turn it must always suppress in favor of its own mythic language of friendship. To put this in stronger terms, perhaps we are witnessing the overturning of an earlier philosophical idealism that invoked friendship as the destination of the political and in its place the emergence of what I will call a nonphilosophical understanding that has determined conflict or war *(pólemos),* even the realization of a perpetual war between the two permanent classes (or populations), which today are represented by the global rich and the global poor, as the ultimate ground from which any future thinking of the political must now depart.[32]

Turning now to address the sense of the second title-phrase, "post-war philosophy," I begin simply by pointing out that this is clearly a misnomer, if only by acknowledging the fact that we have never lived in "a post-war society." In responding to this aporia, however, rather than invoking "a completely new politics" in the manner of Agamben—"that is, a politics no longer founded on the *exeptio* of bare life"—or of "a democracy to come" in the manner of Derrida (an expression that calls for a "militant and interminable political critique"), I simply propose the call for a thoroughly "post-war philosophy." Of course, this raises the question of whether this expression only concerns the "last war" (that is, only the most recent war, including the current war on terror), or the end of war as such—of *all wars,* both archaic and modern, and immemorial—constituting the specific aporia that serves to distinguish my own formulation of the future of political philosophy from the two former ones above, each of which expresses the future according its own specific aporia (that is to say, according to its own idiom and concrete situation). According to my own formulation of a "post-war philosophy," therefore, the fundamental principle of political philosophy would be nothing less than to address the conditions (political, social, economic) in order to finally quit the "state of nature," which in the Kantian sense is equivalent to the state of permanent war. However, Kant also argued that such a departure would need to be preliminary to any higher goal or end (*Zweck*) that could be imagined in the form of a universal political constitution of man or even the complete working out of the "Metaphysics of Justice." In other words, as long as there is war, and even if only a portion of humanity exists in a state of war (i.e., a state of nature), then the whole of humanity would remain without the possibility of justice. Of course, this is no less true today than it was at the end of the eighteenth century, when Kant first made a sketch of this task for the future of philosophy in *Toward Perpetual Peace* (1795) and in the writings that followed outlined a plan for achieving a sustainable peace through the systematic establishment of the principles of politics and a "theory of justice" *(Rechtslehre),* which I will return to discuss in the conclusion.[33] Under its current determination, moreover, one might conclude that the concept of the political has in many respects been reduced to a problem of the "police sciences" *(Poliziewissenschaften),* and I would argue that contemporary philosophy has become far too juridical in its language and major concepts and that today philosophers appear more like the natural lawyers of Kant's own time.

As I argue in the conclusion, we have various avatars of this principle in several contemporary philosophies that substitute the end of actual war with other ends, such as the end of capitalism, the end of humanism, the end of racism and neocolonialism, the end of sexism, the violations of the rights of particular groups, and so on. In his later post-war writings, Antelme gives this principle perhaps its sharpest articulation in addressing the situation of the global poor today who are deprived of all political rights—even the possibility of any claim of future rights. In the face of this growing demographic, as Deleuze and Guattari also observe, there is sufficient evidence to show that "human rights will not save us, nor will a philosophy that is reterritorialized on the democratic state."[34] This is because, as we have witnessed repeatedly in recent years, only the "police can control and manage poverty with the deterritorialization-reterritorialization of shanty towns." Moreover, "what social democracy has not given the order to fire when the poor came out of their territory or ghetto?"[35] Perhaps this is what they mean when they say that modern philosophy has replaced the principle of "rivalry" (the social conflict or antagonism of opinions) with an entirely new affective mood, as we have already recounted around the Heidegger episode, including "weariness," "exhaustion," and even "mistrust." On the one hand, this has to do with the experience of a catastrophe that now lies as a condition of political friendship and even constitutes its "internal presupposition": the shame of being a survivor, which becomes equal to the shame of remaining human in the face of this growing catastrophe.[36] On the other hand, this concerns the repeated attempts on the part of those who seek to conceal themselves from this shame by invoking the moral concepts like desperate alibis or by assigning the different degrees of guilt and distributing justice between victims, executioners, and accomplices. And yet, merely the act of living has become a political decision for everyone today, each of whom has to some unconscious degree become an accomplice to this daily catastrophe, no matter how distant in space and time or how much a particular group might claim to suffer "equally," since as we have seen, the birth of every particular right also brings with it new classes of strangers and those who do not have an allotted share as "co-partners in political rights"*(co-partegeant des droits politiques)*.[37] Once again, recalling Agamben's concept of "bare life," it is the limit-situation of both poverty and terror that the phenomenological meaning of nudity or nakedness that vividly expresses the shame of a being exposed, outside society, without friendship or hospitality. Or, as Arendt has powerfully argued, it is that which distinguishes between those strangers who are "lonely" and "naked" rather than merely "alone." Consequently, there can be no "transitional" or "distributive justice" that will compensate for the universal shame of poverty. If we accept this at the beginning of our philosophy, then the idea of the political philosophy itself must undergo a complete and intensive reevaluation.

In the conclusion of *The Origins of Totalitarianism,* it was also Arendt—who, we recall, was also an astute reader of Kant's later political philosophy—who first proposed the treatment of particular strangers as a foundational site for testing the limits of any current political form of government. Moreover, she argued that the existence of "terror" represents nothing less than "a conscious break" of that *consensus iuris* that, as Cicero argued, was the basis for the concept of a "people," and that, "as international law, in modern times has constituted the civilized world insofar as it remains the foundation-stone of international relations even under the conditions of war."[38] This represents the basis of her most radical thesis concerning totalitarian and all other concepts of law. As she writes:

> Totalitarian policy does not replace one set of laws with another, does not establish its own *consensus iuris,* does not create by one revolution, a new form of legality. Its defiance of all, even its own positive laws implies that it believes it can do without any *consensus iuris* whatever, and still not resign itself to the tyrannical state of lawlessness, arbitrariness, and fear.[39]

Today, and especially in the context of the current war on terror, have we not witnessed the complicity and collusion of the modern democracies with the ongoing perpetuation of this "conscious break with the principle of *consensus iuris,*" even if this break is only partial with regard to certain territories globally and only with respect to international law (for example, in targeting a new class of strangers who, it could be argued, were only created by the "last war")? Who today represents the "tyrannical state of lawlessness" referred to in the above passage, which is equivalent with the Kantian state of nature as the lawlessness that exists between constituted nations, in vast wastelands and in deserts, except the modern terrorist? And yet, as Derrida has also argued, we also find equivalence between the description of the martial character "totalitarian policy" in the passage above and certain "rogue states" who act "in defiance of all" and even *in defiance of their own*

positive laws with which they can believe they can do without.[40] As we
will see, it is basically this same principle of the right of nations that
Kant himself addressed at the end of the eighteenth century as the primary obstruction to the practical realization of a sustainable peace,
since it only "serves to justify those men who are so disposed to seek
one another's destruction and thus to find perpetual peace in a grave
that covers all the horrors of violence and its perpetrators."[41] Today, it
is this same right that remains a blatant contradiction in the very principle of law and that only guarantees, in place of the idea of "perpetual
peace," the ongoing reality of permanent war.

It appears we have now come full circle, a circle that has merely
accelerated to become a vicious cycle. Therefore, in the conclusion I
will propose to cut through this cycle—perhaps even a bit precipitously
in the manner of a Gordian Knot—and return to the claim that the first
principle of any future political philosophy is a critique of actual war,
including the juridical–legal conditions of war, the right of the current
nation-state, the economic and corporate interests involved in the perpetuation of wars, the notion of "just war" *(jus ad bellum)* and the continued threat of nuclear war, as well as other forms of warfare directed
against entire populations (i.e., the scientific and technological region
of "thanatopolitics," strictly defined in its modern senses by Foucault
and Agamben). In response to this global situation, and strictly adher-
ing to Kant's earlier argument (which I will continue to unapologeti-
cally privilege), it is only by "working out" this problem first that a
future philosophy may avail itself of the insight and imagination necessary to work out other problems of reason, leading up to the final problem of a universal constitution of the "human species" (a term that I
employ intentionally for reasons that are explained in chapter 5). Of
course, I realize that many of these claims might sound too fantastic
and far-fetched to be believed (perhaps "a philosopher's sweet dream," or
"an idea fit only for the academy"), but this is founded on the assertion
that one finds in Kant's later political writings that the idea of perpetual
peace should be affirmed as a reality, even if this reality cannot be empirically proven—much less, as Kant says, can it be disproven either—

and therefore it can still function as an a priori idea of reason for any future political philosophy, for which I propose that we begin to substitute the term "post-war philosophy."[42]

To conclude this brief prolegomena, I find it interesting that any proposal to address the actual situation of war is often met with skepticism, as well as claims concerning more generalized but at the same time more specific forms of violence and injustice. However, the most violent forms of inequality and the violation of human rights have historically originated in the conditions of a state of war or have found their forms of specific violence directed against populations and groups through the technologies of war, including genocide, the absence of the rule of law, the restriction or loss of political rights, sexual and racial violence, poverty, famine, hunger, environmental devastation, and the destruction of other species (and, indeed, of all species, in the case of nuclear warfare). Moreover, one does not need to refer to Benjamin's "Critique of Violence," which has been employed lately as Holy Scripture by theorists of sovereignty, including Derrida and Agamben, to distinguish between generalized violence and specific violence as well as the conversion between them. Taking up Deleuze and Guattari's theory of the "planetary war machine," as I discuss in the last section, instead we might ask how a generalized form of violence that already preexists a condition of actual war (e.g., racism, sexism) can be taken up by the war machine to both provide the conditions of an actual state of war (that is, serving as a principle of justification) and also serve as a "direct object" of specific violence that is partly invented by the war machine itself (e.g., genocide, rape warfare). The more crucial distinction, it seems to me, is this moment of actualization (or conversion) between a form of generalized violence and the multiple forms of specific violence occasioned by the invention of new technologies, as well as new juridical and political forms of right, which function to operate this conversion through the actualization of the "concrete situation" of war itself. In turn, it is the concrete situations of war that will provide the conditions of the new forms of generalized violence that will inflict future generations of survivors, as well as serve as the specific conditions for future wars. Here, we might recall that Deleuze and Guattari often complain about the infinite growth of the modern war machine, "like in a science fiction story," which takes two opposing or bipolar directions: the creation of "the most terrible local wars as parts of itself" (i.e., the conversion of a generalized violence into new occurrences of local and specific violence) as well as the creation of "a new type of enemy, no longer another State, nor even another regime, but the 'unspecified enemy'" (i.e., the conversion of a specific form of violence directed against a particular group into a generalized form of violence directed against an unknown and "unspecified" enemy).[43]

In response to these potential objections, therefore, I would simply ask whether we should begin working through these problems by first addressing their root cause in order to begin to ameliorate all the effects that are determined by this cause, which would take the form of a thorough and systematic critique of all the remaining justifications (ethical–moral, political, juridical, religious, etc.) that today continue to determine the political "rights of war" *(jus belli),* including especially the removal of any moral justification that belongs to the notion of "just war," hopefully by the close of the twenty-first century. Another way to put this is that the minute one begins to qualify or to create an exception to the idea of creating the conditions for a permanent and lasting peace, then like the "natural lawyers" of Kant's time as well as in our own, one is immediately led into the ethical dilemma of justifying this or that particular war and thus of ignoring every kind of atrocity and injustice that will inevitably occur in actual wars. This would be the creation of a contradiction in the very concept of right itself, which Kant said ought to be impossible in principle, if you want to preserve the concept of law as being founded on anything more than a purely empirical theory of justice and law, which Kant compares to the fabled wooden head in Phaedrus (i.e., it may be quite beautiful, but unfortunately it has no brain!).[44] In order to resolve this violent contradiction, therefore, philosophically, politically, and sometimes even juridically minded people are left with only two possible choices: either get rid of the principle of law itself as the basis of the concept of right, in which case you remain in a state of war where there can be neither justice nor rule of law; or work relentlessly in order to get rid of the conditions of actual wars, which are responsible for producing the contradiction in the concept of right and justice, in which case you might hope to enter into something that could one day approximate a peaceful—*albeit not necessarily "friendly"*—state of society.

one

Friend (Fr. *l'ami*)

> Without the life of the spirit between friends, we are by our own
> hands outside thought.
>
> —Dionys Mascolo (attributed to Hölderlin), *Autour d'un effort de
> mémoire*

In order to begin our genealogical exercise, first let us return and take
up in more detail the late correspondence between Deleuze and Mascolo. In a letter dated August 6, 1988, Deleuze writes the following in
reply to an earlier letter where Mascolo first raises the possibility that the
basis of philosophical friendship (defined as the "solidarity of thought")
would evoke the concrete situation of a friend who shares a suspicion
concerning thinking itself:

> Your answer was very kind and thoughtful: if there is a secret, it is the
> secret of a thought that is suspicious of thinking, thus a source of con-
> cern *[souci]* that, if found in another person, is the basis of friend-
> ship. . . . Couldn't we reverse the order? Friendship comes first for you.
> Obviously friendship would not be a more or less favorable external
> circumstance, but, while remaining the most concrete, it would be the
> internal condition of thought as such. Not speaking with your friend
> or remembering him or her, etc., but rather go through trials with that
> person like aphasia and amnesia that are necessary for any thinking.
> I no longer remember which German poet wrote of the twilight hour
> when one should be wary "even of a friend." One would go that far, to

wariness of a friend, and all that would, with friendship, put the "distress" in thought in an essential way. I think there are many manners, in the authors I admire, to introduce concrete categories and situations as the conditions of pure thought. Kierkegaard uses the fiancé and the engagement. For Klossowski (and maybe Sartre in a different way), it is the couple. Proust uses jealous love because it constitutes thought and is connected to signs. For you and Blanchot, it is friendship. This implies a complete reevaluation of "philosophy" since you are the only ones who take the word *phílos* literally. Not that you go back to Plato. The Platonic sense of the word is already extremely complex and has never been fully explained. Yet one can sense that your meaning is altogether different. *Phílos* may have been displaced from Athens to Jerusalem, but it was also enhanced during the Resistance, from the network, which are affects of thought no less than historical and political situations. There is already a sizeable history of *phílos* in philosophy of which you are already a part, or, through all sorts of bifurcations, the modern representative. It is at the heart of philosophy, in the concrete presupposition (where personal history and singular thinking combine).[1]

In his reply to Mascolo, Deleuze is responding to the normative view of friendship, one in which supposedly there exists a suspension of other forms of interest and desire (such as the erotic, or the purely egotistic and solipsistic interest) in such a manner that allows the friend to appear to exist beyond suspicion of malevolence. Thus, there is a certain piety that surrounds and protects the person one chooses to call friend, either through discretion or the protection of secrets, as well as the prohibition of overt violence (which, at first, appears to be impossible among friends).

Certainly there can be disagreements, but usually these can be resolved through communication or, most often, suppressed in the name of friendship itself. In other words, it is this special social experience that is concretely lived with others, a form of utopia, that is usually absent from the strife that defines the political sphere, or the sphere of so-called civil society, which is defined by conflicting interests between individuals or classes. Is this by accident, or is this supposed dissymmetry between the strife that defines the political and the utopian experience of friendship itself the ontological reserve of the relationship between these two spheres in Occidental thought? In other words, is not the concrete and everyday experience of the quasi-utopian state shared among friends the very destination of the political idea of friendship, the manner in which the political seems to be destined (to employ a Derridean manner of speaking) from an initial state of war and the conflicting forms of interests between strangers to a final state of union or accord within a society of friends?

Even if it exists primarily as myth or fiction, if what is called the political realm is based on the idea of "free election"—that is, on the idea of friendship as a social determination that is not natural or determined by kinship and the private sphere of the family—then the spontaneous nature of the accord (or alliance) will always be temporal. The specific meaning of temporality has two senses here: first, meaning "not permanent"; second, referring to a spontaneous act or promise that immediately occurs in relation to its past and, in order to exist in the present, must undergo constant repetition. This becomes the basis of the ritual acts of recognition in friendship, which have a profound impact on the particular nature of the accord or alliance in question.

The friend is bound to an oath that is given spontaneously, moreover, becoming the basis for all secret confidences and private communication; because the self in friendship is vulnerable to being exposed to "the Third" (Levinas), this becomes the source of a secret concern that is shared between friends as a mutual limit and source of anxiousness *(souci)*. However, friends do not often speak of this limit—it is avoided, being the repressed condition of their relation that it remain "unthinkable"—but, as often happens, will confess the existence of this limit as the mark of a special protection or confidence. What is this limit? According to Cicero, it is not simply death, but something worse than death—ignominy and hatred.

Why, if mutual love of friends were to be removed, there would be no
single house, no single state that would go on existing; even agriculture
[i.e., economy] would cease to be. If this seems a bit difficult to understand, we can readily see how great the power of friendship and love
by observing their opposites, enmity and ill will. For what house is so
firmly established, what constitution is so unshakable, that it could not
be utterly destroyed by hatred and internal division? From this we may
judge how much good there is in friendship.[2]

In accepting the election of friendship, therefore, I am bound by an
oath to protect the image of the other person *(autrui)* in the place of my
own ego. In some ways this substitution takes the form of an exchange
and becomes partly the basis for the special possessive alterity that defines the friend in some sense as "my other." This is because, from this
point onward, the friend is not *another like all the others* but instead
serves as the condition for protection and alliance. Again, for Cicero,
protection from violence inflicted by others and by time itself is the
condition of the bond of true friendship and even bears the promise of
eternal life for the Roman.

By contrast, what do the above examples of concrete situations and
categories share in common except that they refer to intensive states of
extremity and limit-situations that threaten the social bond: the broken
engagement, the couple who become rivals (or jealous lovers), friends
who are suddenly separated by incredible distances (whether spatial or
psychological) or drawn into an inexplicable trial that threatens to exhaust the possibility of friendship itself. Thus, even though they remain
friends, they find themselves struck dumb by their own passivity and
can only be silent before one another—or, as with Samuel Beckett's
couples, prattle incessantly about their own selfish cares and "needs"
(including the need for friendship itself, or the recovery to friendship).[3]
From these descriptions we can imagine that the concept of friendship
that Deleuze has in mind does not refer to a peaceful state of community, or sharing in common, but rather to the various "limit-situations"
and intensive states of difference that can only occur between friends. It

seems that a state of friendship can only exist within the narrow confines of a social relationship that is already conditioned by the preexist-
ing interests that determine what is "common" becoming the basis of
proximity, identification, and fraternization—but also the implicit conditions of alienation and hostility as well. Consequently, this peaceful
state of bliss and consensus is always haunted by the outbreak of a difference that it cannot pacify, repress, or communicate through, and here
we touch on something of a political problem that can only belong to
friendship, an event that presupposes or occurs only in a state of friendship with its abstract notions of identity and consensus. But who can
say whether this same limit communicates with the limit of the political
itself, whose failure and unconscious repetition belongs to the concept
of friendship that perhaps we have merely "inherited" but which is not
properly founded?

Deleuze refers to these intensive states of difference as "secrets" that
become a constant source of anxiety and intense concern *(souci)* in
friendship, and in a certain sense, it is because they represent the various thoughts of suspicion, rivalry, paranoia, even desire, that each
friend must keep secret from the other, even though these thoughts are
already divided "between friends" and are consequently shared, constituting, perhaps, the positive contents of the unconscious that each friend
bears in anxious concern for the other.[4] There is always an inherent limit
to the friendship hidden within each friend; the sudden revelation of
this limit refers to an event (a word, an action of betrayal, or the refusal
to act in the name of friendship itself) that was always already possible
from the very beginning, even though it may have been previously
unthinkable (i.e., barred from the conscious life that is shared between
friends). If this event remains secret, perhaps it is because it constitutes
a repressed *differend* (to employ Jean-François Lyotard's term), perhaps
even the seed of a catastrophe that would cause the state of friendship
to transform into something else, such as enmity or hatred. It is in this
sense that the event is already virtual, referring to statements that are
unsayable, deeds or actions that are unrealizable, erotic desires that are
unobtainable within the normal limits of friendship—a frequent source

of constant anxiety and care. Above all, this seems to imply that friendship is not a peaceful accord, or form of consensus and equality, but rather a very specific form of strife and conflict that is structured by a social form of *Mitsein* ("being-in-common"), one that enforces a constant vigilance by both parties. Even in the most quotidian relationships defined by friendship there is a secret enmity that could well up at any moment, marking the limit or the end of friendship. Consequently, friends are always suspicious of one another, on the lookout for signs of betrayal of confidences, or worse, the inevitable turning away that marks its extreme limit in death and forgetfulness, like Eurydice's descent into the underworld. Consequently, as Deleuze also suggests, this implicit or virtual conflict is one reason that the friend must be kept under constant surveillance, under careful guard (implying a different motive for proximity than simple amity). Moreover, every statement made by the friend must already contain the unspeakable as its secret condition, almost as if the actual contents of the conversation between friends are only made to paper over the unsaid, something that seems to increase over the duration of the friendship, offering a plausible explanation to why friends often appear to talk endlessly about nothing, or have a habit of saying whatever comes to mind. One might add that friends are very much like philosophers in this respect, and this may even indicate one of the origins of philosophical enunciation.[5]

But what happens when, as Deleuze remarks, "friendship puts the 'distress' in thinking"? Here, distress is no longer merely "concern" or an anxiety over what is already latent in friendship and appearing as its secret reserve, or its outside. Distress indicates a limit-situation, one that occurs when the unspeakable rises to the level of the expressed or the impossible action is realized, interrupting the peace that is normally associated with its semi-utopian state, thus threatening to transform the friend into a rival or an enemy. For example, a friend can suddenly become duplicitous out of a secret source of jealousy or social envy and can seek to damage the image of the friend in the society of others. This becomes an event that could end the friendship through the charge of betrayal. However, here we must ask, a betrayal of what exactly? Perhaps the unspoken rule between friends, that one should always speak positively of the friend and never seek his or her destruction? Is this not the rule that first defines what friendship *ought* to be in its utopian concept, if not in reality? The one betrayed might say: "And I thought you were my friend? And yet, you have been speaking behind my back and plotting my destruction all along." Of course, we all know of those friends who, precisely in the name of friendship itself, will encourage the betrayal of a third friend (especially a lover or fiancé) in order to consolidate their role as "the best friend" and to thus make themselves appear more "proximate," honest, truthful, and therefore ultimately more sincere than the friend or the lover who always ends up failing the ideals of friendship itself. These are just a few of the concrete situations that cause us to think the concept of friendship in "distress." In these situations, the friend is now in the very place to betray the semi-utopia of friendship, either through self-interested cunning or desire, *or perhaps through a secret hatred of the spirit of friendship itself.*

These images might evoke the great figures from William Shakespeare such as Iago or Brutus—a Machiavellian desire, a spirit of revenge, personal envy disguised as the virtues of confidence and true friendship. However, even before Shakespeare's figures, we already have the ancient figure of Medea, who appears in the center of the polis appealing to the virtues of friendship in the course of committing an infanticide. Implicitly, these historical examples also point to the inherent limitation and weakness of friendship as a social bond or as a primitive dyadic form of social organization; it seems the minute that friendship extends beyond its simple dyad—that is, the moment it attempts to constitute a social assemblage comprised of more than two persons—there occurs a re-introduction of the principle of "the Third" and with it all the accompanying possibilities of rivalry and competition over self-interest that is usually deferred to other social relations, especially political ones. Perhaps this is why Deleuze admits the possibility of "malevolence" and violence into the proximity of friendship and asks whether this constitutes the failure of "the friend"—that is, of this or that particular friend, or rather the failure of a certain concept of friendship itself that we have inherited from the Greeks, including the idea of a democratic assemblage of friends that always number more than two individuals, immediately ushering in the possibilities of competition and rivalry and, at its extreme limit, violence and even warfare. In its original situation, such as Deleuze describes it, the friend is introduced into the relationship to knowledge of the Entity; as he writes: "The Greeks violently force the friend into a relationship with the Thing and no longer merely as an extrinsic persona or Other."[6] Thus, it is no longer that the friend appears extrinsic to the Thing's essence but is intrinsic to the very nature of the Thing's revealing and concealing itself, recalling Heidegger's concept of truth as *a-lethia*. In other words, from the Greeks onward, philosophy is no longer a conversation about Things (wisdom), and the presence of the friend is essential to thought being divided from itself and pursuing its unity again by means of the dialectic instituted between equals, each of which functions as both claimant and rival to the Thing's essence. In other words, according to the Greek dialectic of *amphisbetisis,* friendship can only exist through the vigilance of an active and creative will that intervenes in order to mediate all rivalry and competition over an Entity; by shaping and organizing the component interests into aesthetic and ethical expressions of the Beautiful and the Good (or by excluding or repressing certain desires, especially the erotic and purely egotistic instincts, which would transform friendship into something else); and, finally, by turning concern itself into an exercise that requires moral discipline, athleticism and courage, and an aesthetic sensibility of taste capable of appreciating the virtues of perfect friendship. According to this model, friendship becomes an art, which requires of its creators moderation in appetite, sobriety, purification of thought, and, above all, piety, modesty, and respect.[7]

But then, how did "the Greeks" force the friend into the relationship with the knowledge of the Entity, and how would this force not also be experienced as a form of violence that might destroy the possibility of friendship or, at least, confront its real limits? In response, Deleuze asks: "Is this not already too great a task?" In other words, was the ideal of friendship already doomed to fail from its very inception? Would not every friend already be destined to betray the perfection of friendship similar to an athlete who, exhausted, having reached the limit of his or her powers, gives up the race? It would seem here that what is commonly called platonic love is not the only impossible ideal introduced by the Greek philosopher: the idea of friendship may very well be an even greater source of contradiction within Occidental societies. Perhaps in a worst-case scenario we might even suspect that Plato invented these ideals from a spirit of malevolence and bad faith rather than simply from an experience of irony combining his own personal history and singular thinking. Another possibility, no less ironic, is that through the transformation in thinking effected by placing the friend in contact with violence and nonthinking as the extreme limit of our knowledge of the Entity (i.e., the social relation itself), modern philosophy introduces the presence of a dark intentionality or evil spirit *(malin genie)*. Then, immediately following the nineteenth century, the invention of the Unconscious that governs the modern social relation fractures our knowledge of the Entity that is posed between friends; there can be no perfect friendship if my good intentions have been poisoned from the beginning by an unconscious egoism associated with class or race, even gender, allowing for the spirit of malevolence behind all overt acts of faith. The crack widens, eventually encompassing friendship itself in a vast conspiracy that has determined philosophy as merely a form of expression that now belongs to "the history of ideology" (i.e., the externalization of the basic underlying division that determines all social relations).[8]

In response to this history, Mascolo cannot go so far in acknowledging "malevolence" as a possibility that could exist between friends. His concept is still utopian, classical, and not yet modern; or perhaps there is a psychological question of denial that stems from his own personal history that Deleuze, in fact, may be alluding to in his comment concerning his friendship with Robert Antelme and his marriage to Marguerite Duras. Replying to Deleuze's proposal to reverse the condition of distrust, making friendship responsible for putting thought in distress, he expresses a certain amount of anxiety over what this might imply, for if this were the case it would make friendship itself unthinkable.

You suggest a reversal of the proposition, making friendship come first. Friendship would then be put in "distress" in thought. Once again due to distrust, but this time the distrust of friends. But then where would friendship come from? That is a mystery for me. And I cannot imagine what *distrust* (an occasional disagreement, of course, on the contrary— and in an entirely different sense that excludes *malevolence*) is possible of a friend once he or she has been accepted in friendship.[9]

In response, Mascolo seems to argue that the bond of friendship, while always open to occasional disagreement, is, once a friend has been accepted into friendship, not vulnerable to actual malevolence. This would imply that friendship cannot be placed into distress by the friend himself or herself, which would be not merely "unthinkable" but rather an absence of thought (i.e., care, intimate concern, speech, responsibility) that would lead outside of friendship proper. To summarize the lines that Mascolo ascribes to Hölderlin: *Without the life of the spirit between friends, we are by our own hands outside thought.*[10]

Yet, following Deleuze's elliptical assertion, let us admit this at least as a definite possibility—that the friend could, by his or her own hand, do the unthinkable (at least, that which is unthinkable for Mascolo), and would be capable of expressing true malevolence for "the friend." The first thing one would have to cautiously ask is whether, considering this possibility, friendship (at least, in its classical sense) would even be possible any longer. What might the "secret" source of distress be that Deleuze refers to here? Recall the various "concrete situations" that Deleuze invokes to begin constructing his concept of friendship— that is to say, the various couples that do not express the presence of friendship as a bond but rather the limit-situations that constitute its end (betrayal, infidelity, etc). As I have previously suggested, in most familiar experiences of the social bond of friendship, these are the "secret" sources of anxiety: the "limit-situations" that constantly underlie and constitute the unconscious reserve of any friendship. If we have established that the utopian state of society shared between friends implicitly informs the various political idealisms that have been created by

Occidental philosophy—following the Greeks, up to and including the expression of "absolute democracy" (Negri)— then what would be the political consequences for this idealism once we admit into the proximity of friendship the possibility of real malevolence, which in a Christian universe must also include the possibility of evil, or of "doing evil to the friend"? First, there would be no basis for any belief in friendship, for "having faith in one's friend" (which, I might argue, may be a more severe expression of nihilism than any existential or historical experience of atheism).[11] Second, friendship would become "non-Greek," the occasion of a different kind of "concern" than was expressed by the Greek principle of dialectical rivalry between equals *(amphisbetisis)*. Instead, it would be a constant source of suspicion, anxiety, fear, unmitigated or unmediated violence, and, above all, an expression of moral vigilance that is accompanied by neither piety nor aesthetic virtue, but by a different kind of disciplinary spirit altogether—one that most closely approximates the modern character of security and control, in the sense of "keep your friends close but your enemies closer." Accordingly, if the stranger must be kept under constant surveillance, then one must be especially wary of the so-called friend who may be guilty of committing (either in the immanent future, an unknown past, or already in the unconscious present) some unspeakable evil against the friend. Nevertheless, these are the signs of distress in our distressed times, which places any friendship on trial.

In the preface to *The Politics of Friendship*, which I will discuss in relation to the conceptual persona of "the enemy" *(der Feind)*, Derrida stages a grievance or complaint in the name of the unknown friend who has become the victim of a historical crime, in the quasi-juridical sense of an appeal for a wrong that must be righted, a violence to be redressed, similar to Job's complaint against "the voice in the whirlwind."[12] Yet he later asks who would be the appellate court that could be considered qualified to hear the case and to sit in judgment? Not society, which stands in the position of the accused, also in many cases not even one's closest friends, who often turn out to be "miserable comforters." Moreover, are these not just the expressions of a dystopian state of friendship, or the current state of democracy today? If so, we must return to explore the "catastrophe" that is the cause of our modern dystopia of friendship and to what Deleuze calls the affective disturbances of both amnesia and aphasia that this catastrophe introduces between friends. Aphasia is not determined here by the simple form of strife or conflict that causes a lapse or period of silence, as when "friends don't speak with one another for a long time," but rather refers to a more fundamental experience of the loss of a common language of friendship. In turn, amnesia must be understood as more extreme than the simple forgetfulness that occurs between friends as, for example, when they are separated by distance or time. My distance from my former childhood friend is more or less accepted as the inevitable consequence of adulthood, as is the murmur of social anonymity that almost always borders on and threatens any friendship founded by momentary episodes of proximity bounded by space. Thus, the friend emerges from this anonymity only to gradually merge with it again, caught in the ebb and flow that characterizes all social relationships defined by proximity (limited by the conditions of time and space). Normal conceptions of friendship are determined within the limits of permanence and volatility; they are part of what distinguishes "the friend" from other social relationships, such as the relationship with the stranger, the member of the family, or the mere acquaintance. What is particular to the relationship that defines "the friend" is a character of *becoming* that does not seem to belong to these other relationships.

Yet the experience of real amnesia or aphasia can never be imagined to belong to friendship, unless by the intervention of some catastrophe or by an "outside" force that first appears as violence. I would argue at this point that a state of war becomes applicable as a possible causality, in the name of "catastrophe." This seems to be what Deleuze refers to under Mascolo's concept of the friends of the Resistance, which he says fundamentally changes the Greek concept of friendship into something distinctly modern, a change that is philosophical as much as it is historical and political and that, in turn, demands that the concept of *phílos* be completely rethought. He writes: "*Phílos* may have been displaced from

Athens to Jerusalem, but it was also enhanced during the Resistance, from the network, which are affects of thought no less than historical and political situations."[13] Thus, the militant idea of the friend (or "comrade") necessarily includes the possibility of "distress" *and* "betrayal" as the very conditions of friendship, understood in this context as the occasion of secret confidence, or a common goal of association. This is something that the Greeks would never have imagined, since they did not place friendship directly into a relation to war, whereas the modern notion of "the friend" already includes this relation in the opposition between "the friend" and "the enemy" as Schmitt has already argued in *The Concept of the Political,* where we find the following statement: "War as the most extreme political means discloses the possibility which underlies every political idea, namely, the distinction between friend and enemy."[14]

Rather than tracing this distinction through the political philosophy of Schmitt (I will return to Schmitt in chapter 2), I prefer instead to turn to the political theory of Karl Marx and Friedrich Engels, who fundamentally transformed the original Greek concept of friendship by defining the situation of friends in a distinctly modern sense of war, a war between two classes of society, or the "war between the two estates." At the same time, Marx-Engels also draw on the same Greek source by defining communism as an absolute gregarious spirit of a society, "the friendship of the proletariat." Therefore, within the private sphere of the civil society Marx placed all the contradictions that divide the human species *(Geschlecht)* into different classes; however, he situated the concept of friendship firmly in the political sphere. Furthermore, it is important to note that for Marx friendship would no longer function dialectically to mediate rivalry and competition between individuals and classes, since this belonged to an earlier political form that itself is only a product of a previous "self-alienation" *(Selbstentfremdung)* of the species. As Marx writes, "The possessing class and the proletarian class represent one and the same human self-alienation."[15]

In other words, what would be the basis for political friendship except that of pursuing one's own "private interests" in the public sphere of the civil society? Since rivalry and competition are only the effects of an original division and the dialectic of friendship (or democracy), they only serve to mitigate and pacify the fundamental contradictions that afflict society. A classless society, however, would be defined by the cancellation of this division and all its consequent differences in the creation of one "species-being" that would henceforth *share the same conditions of social existence*. For such a species, the very condition of friendship will have changed along with the meaning of the political, which would necessarily disappear along with the division between the political state and civil society. There may be a utopian politics, but there can be no politics in utopia, since this would represent a fundamental contradiction that is supposedly erased (or sublated) by Communism, which cancels out the partial class interests that define the political. Ironically it is only from the condition of the historical present, a perspective that Marx saw clearly, only the state of total war that approximates such a situation, when the internal contradictions of society take on an externalized form of *real* contradiction between two apparent species-beings. In response to the question "Who is the friend?" Marx will write only the one who shares with me the same conditions of social existence, for every other social species is my enemy. Thus, the term "comrade" bears the militant idea of an ally in a struggle or war as well as the social idea of the friend who is linked to a bond that is not inherited, or natural, but rather is contrived by the introduction of an artificial form of inequality between social relations that will become a source of constant concern *(souci)*. In this case, according to a Marxist materialist practice, concern is defined by "action" and by the labor of negativity (critique) in which all existing social relations, including the social relationship of friendship, are exposed to a process of *becoming* that Jean-Paul Sartre once compared to being dipped in a bath of sulfuric acid, stripping away their dross and ideological façades and perhaps revealing at the end of this historical process the face of the only *true* friend.[16]

Here it should be obvious that the nature of this concern *(souci)* must be understood completely differently from its earlier political manifestations, since it was Marx who was perhaps the first to announce that it is precisely the appeals to universal friendship or fraternity that one must be especially wary of in a time of war, since "the friend" could in fact turn out to be the worst "enemy." In other words, as he and Engels warned many times, the very principle of democratic friendship must be suspected of harboring the greatest chances for betrayal. For example, this principle of treachery is clearly outlined by Marx and Engels in their 1850 *Address to the Communist League,* where they write:

> At the present moment, when the democratic petty bourgeois are everywhere oppressed, they preach in general unity and reconciliation to the proletariat, they offer it their hand and strive for the establishment of a large opposition party which will embrace all the different shades of opinion in the democratic party, that is, they strive to entangle the workers in a party organization in which general socialist democratic phrases predominate, behind which their special interests are concealed and in which the particular demands of the proletariat may not even be brought forward for the sake of beloved peace.[17]

Of course, we can easily imagine that one of the "general socialist democratic phrases" to which Marx and Engels are referring was the phrase of friendship, which they warn must be "most decisively rejected."[18] It is also here that we might be addressing something comparable to the network of the Resistance that Deleuze refers to in his letter to Mascolo as profoundly transforming the concept of friendship through a concrete and historical situation of war. What both situations demonstrate is the fact that the very principle of democratic friendship was to be distrusted, even to the point of representing malevolence and treachery. One could not be a friend to the petty bourgeois and a friend of the proletariat any more than, as Deleuze suggests in reference to Mascolo's own experience in the Resistance, "a friend to the SS" and "a friend to the Resistance." It is only from the overt differences in the historical and political situations that one contradiction would appear to be more extreme than the other; in reality, however, they represent the same contradiction between "the friend" and "the enemy," creating an extreme antithesis that cannot be resolved dialectically, which is to say, *neither* by philosophy *nor* by politics.

Only the acceptance of a state of permanent war will bring this dialectic to the point of an extreme antithesis, in which the two opposing identities are finally split apart, producing the threat of an unmediated and generalized violence that becomes too great for the idealistic aspirations of any political ideal of friendship, which can no longer serve as the principle for mediating new social antagonisms produced by this overdetermined form of contradiction. If the Greeks had been successful for a time, according to Deleuze, in forcing friendship into a certain relation to violence (though by excluding actual violence to another sphere altogether, to a space that lies outside the political sphere), the appearance of this new antagonism becomes too great for this archaic concept of friendship, which falters or fails to reconcile this opposition or, as Deleuze says in a very telling remark, becomes "exhausted," too weak, or too traumatized to maintain the relationship between different claimants and rivals together in a common accord. Of course, in this description Deleuze is also referring to the dispersion of the city (pólis) as the designated open space *(agorá)* for these great athletic contests and tragic battles; instead, this space becomes identified with "the world" and at the same time becomes "molecular" and indiscernible, merging with other, formerly peripheral, spheres and can no longer can be gathered and centralized.

According to this final development of the state form, one can invoke Foucault's thesis concerning modern forms of biopower that exceed the earlier spaces in society reserved for the visible exercise of sovereign power. In response to the appearance of this new form of social contradiction, to employ a classical Marxist terminology, new techniques are forged that assume all the hallmarks of the brutal forms of domination and subjugation that characterize modern so-called political programs, as well as new forms of subjective processes that are more submerged within the so-called private spheres of social life (such as the everyday subjective experiences of racism or sexism, for example). It is precisely at this point, as Deleuze recounts in his latest writings on Foucault, that we witness a transition from earlier disciplinary society to what he calls a "society of control," since the principle of control is itself premised on a realization of the unmediated nature of the primary contradiction of society itself, as Marx had earlier defined it, and consequently its submission to a series of transformations that seek *not* to resolve this contradiction—*actually, today this conflict is deemed to be permanently irresolvable*—but rather *to cause it to change into something else* so that, if it cannot be canceled out *(aufgehoben),* at least it can be better managed or controlled!

two

Enemy (Ger. *der Feind*)

The king who is situated anywhere immediately on the circumference of the conqueror's territory is termed the enemy.

—Kautilya, *Arthashastra*, book VI, *The Source of Sovereign States*

We began with an image of the friend "who places thinking in distress" and concluded that this marks the exhaustion of the earlier Greek concept of "friend" *(phílos)*, an exhaustion of its original sources that can be detected in a tradition of post-war continental philosophy, particularly in France, that no longer departs from the earlier Greek sources of *philein* and *philía* but rather from the philosophies of Marx and Friedrich Nietzsche. By the term "post-war" I am referring not only to the historical period of post-war societies—that is, the period we continue to be in the process of quitting, but have not yet left, a period that makes of us all, in a very strange way, either survivors or deportees—but also to the overturning of the Platonic ground of an earlier philosophical idealism that invoked friendship as the destination of the political and the emergence in its place of what I will call a nonphilosophical understanding that has determined war *(pólemos)*, even "permanent war," as the ultimate ground from which any realistic understanding of the concept of the political must depart. Consequently, it is for this reason that we should immediately turn to the concept of "the enemy" *(der Feind)* that has re-surfaced in the recent commentary around the writings of Carl Schmitt, especially those offered by Agamben and Derrida.

As we know from several recent commentaries on *The Concept of the Political* (1932), and those by Agamben and Derrida in particular, Schmitt focuses almost exclusively on what he calls "the concrete situations" of the determination of the enemy relationship in order to arrive at what he claims to be a pure concept of the political as being first of all founded on the need to determine the friend–enemy distinction as a point of certainty that structures the social field—that is, the need to identify the enemy of my friend and the friend of my enemy. In his reading of Schmitt, which I will return to in greater detail below, Derrida is completely accurate in determining the character of this certainty as not an epistemological certainty but rather a practical certainty *(prâxis)*, which is why Schmitt calls it a "concrete situation," referring to the nature of the knowledge to the subject who knows, who is capable of acting and in this case, referring to one who is capable of knowing and acting on "who is the enemy" and "who is the friend" from among all social relationships in which the subject is situated. As Derrida writes:

> If the political exists [in Schmitt's sense], one must know who everyone is, who is a friend and who is an enemy, and this knowing is not a mode of theoretical knowledge but one of practical identification: knowing consists in knowing how to identify the friend and the enemy.[1]

As could also be demonstrated regarding the praxis demanded by a Marxist determination of "scientific materialist practice," as the result of which the recognition of the "friend–enemy" couple first becomes an acute political problem, lending credence to Schmitt's analysis. In other words, something striking occurs when we realize that in both concepts of the political—that of Schmitt and that of Marx—the fundamental order of determination is first focused on the enemy. The enemy comes first, prior to the friend, in the order of this distinction; it is only after the enemy is determined that the relations to friends (or comrades) is made possible. It is the certainty of the identity of the enemy that first allows for the "recognition" of the friend (i.e., *the enemy of my enemy is my friend*). In a certain manner, this already fulfills Schmitt's argument that the polemical character that determines the concept of the political in a nonphilosophical sense is a pragmatic or concrete situation of alliances in a more or less generalized situation of war, something that can also be found in Marx's concept of the political in accordance with the image of generalized (or international) class warfare, which also follows the changing conception of war itself as a form of conflict that exceeds the earlier boundaries of nation and territory and, by the end of the nineteenth century, enlists entire populations and "races."

In the case of Schmitt's concept of the political, however, this allows for the emergence of the modern state to appear as the purest and most instrumental determination of the friend–enemy distinction; in a Hegelian sense, we are conscious of the certainty of the state's identity and the political by its function to wage war on the basis of this distinction. It is in relation to the state and its power to determine the enemy that the subject becomes conscious of the political as such. The importance of Marx was to have recognized the certainty of both this identity and this power and to turn their instrumental function into a weapon that could be wielded by the working classes in their own national spheres. Marx "demythologized" this identity by revealing that "the state" was itself only a "modern machine" invented by a certain class, one that could in turn be turned against them. In order for this to happen, a new class-consciousness needed to emerge that would find itself directly in opposition to the certainty of the political founded on the nation-state. The certainty of national identity, by which the friend–enemy distinction was determined by the different national classes of bourgeoisie competing for their own particular class interests through the political instruments they had invented, would need to be replaced by the "concrete situation" of a new universal class at war against all national elites, who in the end would be revealed to be only the different bourgeoisie *each in its own sphere of influence,* all having an integral role to play in the states they have instituted to pursue their own particular interests. However, for our purposes it is important to notice that this is a radical overturning of the original Greek concept of the polis as the common or open space *(agorá)* that is shared by friends who must organize the form of conflict *(stásis)* into generalized forms of competition *(philoti-mia)* that do not approach the extreme division implied by war *(pólemos)*. Let us be clear on this point, however: war *(pólemos)* is still a distribu-tion or partition of space (even when this distribution takes the form of occupation or colonization), as well as the economic distribution of goods (even through their destruction). Nevertheless, it is this distribu-tion or economy that Plato sought to keep "outside" the polis, admitting only those specific forms of antagonism and violence that originally belonged to the term *stásis,* which is why the Greek term indicates both equality and strife; therefore, it is the identity of these two opposing and contradictory meanings that form a specific dialectical trajectory for the history of the polis to resolve.

As Leo Strauss has already observed in his epilogue to the 1976 re-edition of *The Concept of the Political,* one of the distinctive charac-teristics that he finds in Schmitt's analysis of the political is that, unlike other regions of culture and society, *the political has no sphere of its own.*[2] In other words, the friend–enemy grouping can be found in other spheres and regions of "culture" (civil society) such as the religious, economic, legal, scientific, and ethical. However, it is only the political that names the point of actuality and "concrete determination" of a par-ticular friend–enemy grouping at a given historical moment. Religious conflicts can intensify within or between societies, but they become political only to the extent that they threaten to become actualized as lethal conflicts, empowering each side with the power to kill or to sacrifice the members of their own association. Although it would seem that Schmitt is founding the political on the actuality of war—a thesis that is more in keeping with that of Foucault—he reminds us many times that it is not the actuality of war that proves to be most decisive in determining the political but rather a purely virtual decision that lies at the basis (or the ground) of the "right to kill," even though this ground will have no grounds of its own, and will hang suspended and in abey-ance, as if waiting to be justified or officially sanctioned by a form of sovereignty, even if this justification appears on the most arbitrary or natural of grounds, such as self-defense or "might makes right."

The political, then, would be the purest expression of a decision to kill and it is for this reason that it has no separate sphere of its own; rather, it lies beneath every sphere of culture, every religious argument, every quarrel between neighbors, every encounter with a stranger, in every murderous impulse or genocidal thought. However, in all these expressions it is without the power to actualize itself—that is, to become decisive. The political would simply be the name for the "concrete situation" of a decision once it has been made; it would come after the thought of killing, but before the actual act of killing. It would become not only possible but also a form of potentiality that can be realized at any moment afterward, and in this sense we can understand the nature of this decision as something that divides time into a "before" and an "after" and institutes itself as a ground for the future determination. It is only in this way that we might understand Schmitt's clarification that "the State must presuppose the political" in the sense that the state emerges from the ground of a decision to kill, which then subsequently must also be deprived of its simple moral meaning for the individual. Rather, it must first be purified of all psychological motives so that it can then appear sanctioned, legalized, excused, ordered, justified, rationalized, and condoned. If, for Georg Wilhelm Friedrich Hegel, the state represents the specific historical entity of the community's *consensus iuris,* according to Schmitt, it does so only as bearing all the responsibility for the community's decision to kill on behalf of the community itself (to preserve, to protect, and even to expand or to subjugate other communities in its own interest). At the same time, the personality of the state must assume all the consequences and the risk for the decision to kill, including the risk of provoking sacred violence in which the state itself would become the divine victim and scapegoat. In other words, the state assumes the position and historical consciousness of a Master who enters into a life-and-death struggle over recognition and prestige *(fama),* and the wilderness of history is replete with the epic examples of individuals (such as Agamemnon) who were condemned for seeking personal immortality, becoming instead the divine goats who wander through the wilderness of eternal ignominy.

And yet, if Schmitt derives his theory of the state from Hegel, he clearly departs from Hegel by so narrowly cauterizing the character of the decision on which the personality of the state is grounded. Although for Hegel the state represents the conscious decision of the community to bring itself into existence as a subject—as an emanation of the desire of consciousness itself to become embodied in an entity—he would not so narrowly define the consciousness of negation as the power of annihilation of the subject who stands opposed to the I, since for Hegel, negation takes on many forms, only some of which take the form of negating the other I in itself in order to restore the subject to its own certainty. For Schmitt, however, it seems that the specific negation that stands for the concept of the political is *nihil negativum*. In other words, Schmitt is thinking as a jurist and not as a philosopher. And therefore, as in jurisprudence, he strictly determines the deciding issue on the existence of a precedent that will function as a rule for each "concrete situation" in which the political appears as the condition of the entity of the state. As we noted earlier, moreover, the rule that Schmitt claims is *jus belli*: "The right to demand from its own members the readiness to die and to unhesitatingly kill its enemies."[3] It is on the basis of this rule that the concept of the political can be purified of all the murkiness to which it has been subjected by romantic philosophy and by liberal humanists alike. It becomes similar to Ockham's razor in the sense that it allows Schmitt to identify precisely the transformation of cultural association into political association (for example, religious association into a political entity) and thereby becomes the basis for the emergence of new and separate entities in the geopolitical sphere, in some way similar to Kant's representation of nations as unique "moral individuals."[4]

If Schmitt narrows and cauterizes, in a certain sense, Hegel's theory of the state, it is not the case that he simply invents a new definition or merely reduces all existing definitions to one rule, the rule of *jus belli,* for the sake of ease. In point of fact, I would argue that Schmitt actually derives his precedent from the concrete situation in the history of law itself, which is decisive in transforming the nature of *jus belli* and its relationship to sovereignty. This situation is that of the Roman

Imperium, where the rule of *jus belli* is exclusively claimed by the personality of the state (Caesar and his procurators) in the situation of its sovereignty and imperial jurisdiction. One of the distinctive features of Roman law was the separation of Roman imperial sovereignty from the cultural and religious sovereignty of subjected peoples or "nations" *(ethnē),* which were defined as *politeuma* (a term that later signifies "commonwealth" but officially serves to designate a "colony," particularly a colony of foreigners, within the urban precincts of the polis).[5] Subjected peoples placed under the jurisdiction of Roman sovereignty through war and imperial conquest could still maintain their ethnic identity, their religious and cultural laws, and even certain aspects of their political personality (usually in the form of the despot or rulers); however, as the price of preserving their separate identity and distinctive personality as a people or culture, subjected colonized peoples had to sacrifice to the Roman sovereignty two things that would be essential to the preservation of a completely independent form of sovereignty: the right to kill or to make war and a willingness to martyr themselves for the preservation of their own sovereignty. It is here we see the separation of the political from *jus belli* and perhaps the very beginning of the creation of a modern concept of the political that is deprived of the very sovereignty on which the identity of the modern state can appear as a distinctively separate entity based on the "right to kill."

We can illustrate the function of Roman imperial law by referring to the early Christian gospels surrounding the crucifixion of Jesus of Nazareth and to Flavius Josephus's account in *The Antiquities of the Jews.* In both sources, we have the representation of a distinct *politeuma* (the Jewish people), which is represented by the religious tribunal of the Sanhedrin, on one side, and by the sovereignty of King Herod, on the other. Between these authorities, and transcending both, is Pontius Pilate, the Roman Procurator of Judea who is charged with the garrison in Jerusalem. In the midst of these different authorities, a man is brought to the Sanhedrin under a charge of violating the Jewish religious laws; after a hearing a decision "is made to execute this man, Jesus of Nazareth." However, having no power to act on this decision, the man must be brought before the Roman authority Pilate, who is the only authority invested with the power to confer on this decision an official sanction that will result in the execution of this man. Upon questioning this man, initially Pilate finds no claim that could support the exercise of his right to kill; basically, Pilate does not identify Jesus as "an enemy of Rome." Although he has become a popular religious leader, he has not incited war or claimed for himself *jus belli,* which would place him in the position of a sovereign enemy. At the same time, Pilate perceives a tricky situation among his own *politeuma,* and so he defers his own decision to the Jewish king, Herod. In other words, he grants a "state of exception" to Herod, and this implies that Pilate temporarily gives to Herod the power of capital punishment but only to exercise in this concrete situation and in this case only. However, Herod perceives the trap set for him and redirects this authority back to Pilate, invoking the terms of Roman law that it would be a violation of his own authority to exercise this power even just once. Pilate is once more at a loggerheads and decides once more to exercise a state of exception and to offer an actual "enemy of Rome," one of the Sikarites (so-called freedom fighters or terrorists) who has committed political murder and who was already under Pilate's ban of death, thinking that the people would agree with him concerning who is the greater enemy of Caesar and spare the life of Jesus from this decision. According to the narrative of John, the people choose the other man, and the elders threaten that if he does not condemn Jesus, then he will prove himself to be "no friend of Caesar" (John 19:12).[6]

According to the different versions of the episode from the gospel literature, various new evidence is brought in to justify this decision, including that Jesus ordered the people to stop paying taxes and that some people have been calling Jesus "King of the Jews," which would directly violate Roman rule, since the people already have King Herod, who has been identified by Roman authorities as the only legitimate sovereign personality of the people by blood. Thus, fearing that a popular appearance of a second king, a king identified as the return of the archaic personality of David, who would liberate Israel and restore her sovereignty under God's rule rather than Caesar's, Pilate agrees under the weight of this new piece of evidence to identify Jesus of Nazareth as an enemy of Rome and to order his execution outside the gates of the city, along with other criminals and enemies of the domestic peace, or *Pax Romanum.* According to the legend, therefore, Jesus is crucified and one of the garrison soldiers nailed a placard above his corpse bearing the sentence IESVS NAZARENVS REX IVDÆORVM (also translated into Greek and Hebrew) as the name of the capital offence.

From this example we might immediately confirm the validity of Schmitt's thesis that the power of the state rests on the various mechanisms that flow from *jus belli,* including the legal–juridical power to rule in the case of identifying the enemy who is subject to the sentence of death. And yet, the very nature of the example already reveals a "state of exception" that could not logically be assumed to apply to all incarnations of the state, either past or present, given the fact that this example belongs to a particular imperial formation, which one would expect might only be applied to situations of colonization, occupation, or territories secured and administered as "tributes" of war. Of course here what I am implying has already been suggested by Marx (and can be found encrypted in Schmitt as well), that the theory of the modern state is thoroughly derived from the juridical and political institutions adapted from the period of the Roman Empire, including the exclusive reservation of the right to make war, and that the personality of sovereignty is no longer a "temporary state of exception" (in a situation of colonization or postbellum occupation) but rather should be regarded as a permanent feature of sovereign state power. Perhaps this would go a long way in explaining the contamination between the two senses of conflict noted above, between *pólemos* and *stásis,* as well as various confusions that occur between the determinations of the public and private enemy but particularly the confusion of the form of violence pertaining to the inside/outside—that is, between internal and external precincts of the polis, the former being subject to the dialectic of the political and the latter being circumscribed as belonging to the conditions of total war against one who is judged to be "a natural enemy of the state." For example, in a post-9/11 world, it might serve to outline the archaic imperial grounds of the various justifications for war made by the Bush administration against an "enemy" who, according to the definition offered by Schmitt, has decisively demonstrated "the readiness to die and to unhesitatingly kill its enemies."[7] Ironically, according to Schmitt's own logic, if the concept of the political can be understood to appear in its purest and most threadbare sense in the current "war on terror," it is because any moral sense of evaluation (i.e., that of a "just war") must be assumed to already express a polemical or oppositional meaning and cannot be employed theoretically or scientifically to grasp the truth of the situation.

Again, it is from this "concrete situation" that we might now return to the original context of *The Republic,* where the determination of civil conflict *(stásis)* is set apart from a more violent opposition with a "natural enemy": the war *(pólemos)* between the Greek and the "barbarian" *(barbaros).* In other words, the character of the friend–enemy distinction can only emerge from within the Greek polis in which there is a tacit identity that unifies opposites in the form of conflict and that can then be submitted to the specific labor of the dialectic to unify opposites on the basis of a produced recognition of identity. This distinction can only occur among Greeks, or between Greeks, and can never be extended to encompass the form of antagonism between Greek and barbarian, who Plato defines as "one who is naturally an enemy." This is a point that Schmitt notes in passing early in *The Concept of the Political,* and it is odd that he does not spend any time dealing with the contradiction that it implies.[8] This is because the practical decision concerning "who is the enemy" in the case of the barbarian does not belong to the concept of the political but occurs "naturally" and thus remains outside it (just as the Greek term refers to the lawless area outside the precinct of the city). For Plato, according to Schmitt's note, it was unthinkable for such an antagonism to occur between civil identities, since "a people cannot be at war with itself," which is why civil war may not be understood as a creative conflagration (or the creation of a new sovereign people) according to Plato's argument. The barbarian, however, names a "natural enemy," either through inheritance or designation, and of course, Plato here is referring to the Persians who are the natural enemies of the Greeks. The very existence of the barbarian is a natural antithesis to everything Greek; such an antithesis cannot be resolved politically but only by total war that seeks to "exterminate all the Brutes!" according to the famous line by Colonel Kurtz in Joseph Conrad's *Heart of Darkness*.[9] This would seem to imply, however, that the friend–enemy distinction is secondary to this more archaic determination of the opposition Greek–Barbarian: as an "exception" that must be excluded from any purely political determination of civil hostility, even though it may continue to persist as a "natural metaphor" that can be employed in a polemical sense of "winning the hearts and minds." Therefore, given the nonpolitical origin of the friend–enemy grouping, rather than attempting to erect a pure concept of the political on the grounds of an impure distinction (which is already present in Plato), perhaps instead we should question the basis of this "other enemy" who arrives by nature and who never belongs to the dialectic of the political *as such*.

It is at this point that we now turn to Derrida's relentless attack on Schmitt's purity of the concept of the political in his deconstruction of all of Schmitt's claims to purify the term "politics" from every weakened, mixed, abstract, and metaphorical sense (economic, religious, aesthetic, and even moral). In the several commentaries on Schmitt in *The Politics of Friendship*, Derrida argues that these claims are founded on an impure presupposition (if not prejudice) of "the political as such" in a Platonic sense. This is most clearly argued in a note that appears in his chapter "On Absolute Hostility," where Derrida recounts the transcript of Schmitt's interrogation by the American prosecutor at Nuremburg, Professor Robert Kempner. When asked about a sentence in which Schmitt asserts that "Jewish authors" were not responsible for the creation of a theory of space (*Raun*), nor indeed for "the creation of anything at all," Kempner asks: "Do you deny that this passage is in the purest Goebbels' style?" Schmitt replies, "In its intent, method, and formulation, it is a pure diagnosis . . . a scholarly thesis that I would defend before any scholarly body in the world."[10] Here we see the word "pure" employed in Schmitt's own discourse in a manner similar to how it is used not only in *The Concept of the Political* but also with regard to Schmitt's original intent, method, and formulation in this scholarly work. It would seem that this scene, to Derrida's mind at least (and here I am only speculating), has so contaminated the usage of this term as to make suspect any claim to the neutral (i.e., scientifically objective, or "purely diagnostic") status of his discourse. As Derrida writes: "He [Schmitt] would wish—it is his Platonic dream—that this 'as such' should remain pure at the very spot where it is contaminated."[11] It is no accident, then, that Derrida frequently evokes "a Schmittian-style discourse" (perhaps an allusion to the previously cited phrase by Kempner, "in the purest Goebbels' style").

Recalling again the passage in Plato's *Republic* on which Schmitt's own argument heavily relies, where Plato attempts to exclude the stranger from the boundaries of the polis, Derrida alludes to the long tradition of historical scholarship on this passage to show that Plato is here himself engaged in a polemic, or diatribe, one that seeks to remove the political possibilities of real war from "civil war." As Schmitt himself acknowledges in a note on the passage, "Civil war is only a self-laceration and does not signify perhaps that a new state or people is being created."[12] As Derrida rightly observes, "The purity of the distinction between *stásis* and *pólemos* remains in the *Republic* a paradigm, accessible only to discourse."[13] The conceptual distinction is only accessible through the metaphors that Plato employs to establish the difference between "killing the enemy" and "self-laceration." In other words, for Plato civil war is tantamount to an act of misrecognition or misidentification in which one thinks one is aiming at an enemy only to shoot oneself instead. In politics as in war, the problem of "friendly fire" is an ever-present threat, and it is crucial to know "who the enemy is" and practically "how to recognize the other who is the enemy" in order to avoid mistaking the enemy for oneself (or one's friend). To assist in this process of identification, Plato employs the analogy of the barbarian (or one "who is an enemy by nature") in order to orientate this distinction outward in an appropriate direction, away from the polis, and also, metaphorically or poetically, away from one's own body or the body proper of the people itself and toward the foreign body of the *hostis*. In other words, Plato employs the paradigm of "barbarian vs. Hellene" to assist his Greek audience in conceptually orienting this distinction between proper and improper identification, even though he then worries about the metaphorical properties of this analogy when applied to antagonisms internal to the polis. Returning to Schmitt's use of this identification and for the mechanism of identification at the basis of the political decision of "who is the enemy?" how can this purely political determination be made on the basis of an analogy to one "who is the natural enemy?" which is to say, on the basis of an impure, prepolitical determination? Race would only be one concept that has emerged in the modern and colonial world on the basis of this analogy, perhaps in order to orient social antagonisms toward a foreign body, but others no less problematic have preceded it. In fact, we know that the entire history of the concept of the political is plagued by the inappropriate, or metaphorical, uses of this analogy, especially in the politico-strategic uses of "the natural enemy" up to and including the strategic use deployed by Marx and Engels when they identified the bourgeoisie as the natural enemy of the proletariat. Perhaps this is enough to throw into sharp relief Derrida's criticism of Schmitt's constant claim of purifying the concept of the political from all abstractions (by which he means of all weak analogies) and the friend–enemy concepts from all metaphor and symbol, when the concept of the enemy is impure from the start—that is to say, a bastard concept.

In concluding my brief observations, one would naturally want to ask, what of the friend in all of this? Of course, if I have spent a lot of time talking about Schmitt's enemy concept, this is because the enemy naturally comes first in the order of determination, and even in Plato the clear identification of the enemy helps to determine the direction in which one will look for one's friends: the friend dwells inside the city, close to one's own proper body, or one's kind, toward whom one may bear a certain envy that even approaches enmity (in a psychological sense) but doesn't approach hostility or open warfare. In other words, beginning with the "concrete situation" of the enemy, we are led in a certain direction toward the friend, but the identity of the friend

remains equally abstract, either deferred to a future when one has complete practical knowledge concerning who all of one's friends are or
deflected to a private and interior space that dwells closest to one's own
body (in its very nakedness), where the friend assumes a nonpolitical
determination of proximity with the self. Perhaps this sense of privation, which surrounds the identity of the friend almost like an aura, is
constitutive of the concept as well. And yet, is friendship the result of
the same forms of identification by which the enemy is determined,
or is it the case that in the paradigm of the friend–enemy only one term
is more concrete and recognizable than the other? Moreover, we know
that the modern state has developed a vast and constantly self-updating
technology of identification (from the issuing of papers, birth certificates, social security numbers, passport photos, verified signatures and
fingerprints, digital passwords, retinal scans, DNA encodings, etc.),
which, according to Schmitt's thesis, are all telescoped onto the friend–
enemy grouping. And yet, is there not a fundamental dissymmetry in
the history of corollary technology for the identification of the friend?
If such technologies exist, I am not certain what these might be—what
or who operates them? Perhaps as a result of this lack of equivalent
development by the institutions of state power, the concept of the friend
remains no less of an abstraction, but for different reasons. For while
in every given political society, today or historically, there is a general
agreement (or consensus) concerning "who is the enemy?" there can
only be multiple and highly variable responses to the question "who is
the friend?" Perhaps this is Schmitt's basic premise as to why in the
friend–enemy grouping the enemy always appears more "concrete,"
more knowable, than the friend, and for that reason it is more useful
for political differentiation—useful, as I have underlined, in a practical
manner, as a form of political praxis. Therefore, the enemy is always
a "public enemy" who can become the subject of state propaganda
and revolutionary treatises alike; whereas the friend always remains a
nebulous and completely "underdeveloped" concept.

This is the very problem that Derrida invokes in the following passage from the chapter "In Human Language, Fraternity," where he asks,

"If a politics of friendship rather than war were to be derived, there would have to be agreement on the meaning of 'friend.' However, the signification of 'friend' can only be determined from within the friend/enemy opposition."[14] What Derrida is calling our attention to in this passage is that the signification of the term "friend" is itself fated to remain abstract within a system—linguistic, juridical, and social—that is ordered by the nearly univocal agreement of the term "enemy" *(der Feind)*. In other words, it is not that the friend suffers from a lack of signification, but rather from too much signification, which is determined in various different manners such as individualistic, subjective, intuitive, culturally relative, probabilistic, spontaneous, and overdetermined. Here we might turn briefly to the philosophy of Deleuze in order to diagnose the failure of the concept of the friend to achieve the sense of a "concrete situation" in the Schmittian sense. Again, we must note in Schmitt that the literalness of the enemy designation exactly corresponds to the concreteness of the political signification; war *(pólemos)*, whether virtual or actual, is precisely the point from which all social divisions are ordered into a hierarchy in which the state merely emerges as the operator of the most concrete realization of the friend–enemy designation. Today, from the popular culture of science fiction, we can only imagine that peace will be possible with the appearance of an enemy who threatens the life of the species, and yet this can only be viewed as the projection of our own peculiar friend–enemy concept onto other forms of life. It is not by coincidence that in the genre of science fiction the contemporary hero of these popular myths usually justifies the act of extermination with some ideological version of anthropocentrism, racism, speciesism, or even sexism, in the same language as earlier historical representatives. For example, in response to the moral claim that appears in *Aliens,* "You can't just choose to exterminate an entire species," one of the protagonists exclaims: "Yeah, just watch me!" In other words, *"exterminate them all!"*

Here I simply point to these two forms of abstraction that surround and determine the concepts of both the friend and the enemy, which should not be considered as an opposition of two pure social identities but rather as two forms of social differentiation of self and other—according to Deleuze and Guattari's terminology, one molar and the other molecular. It is clear that the "enemy" is molar in the sense that it appears as the most abstract determination (i.e., lacking individuation) of both the self and the other. According to Schmitt, Hegel conceived of the concept of the enemy in its purest sense as "the negation of otherness in the self." The enemy, therefore, would be the site of an undifferentiated otherness, which would be stripped of all its traits of individuation save one: that of being opposed to an equally undifferentiated self. Thus, the enemy is the most reductive and abstract form of differentiation, a differentiation that lacks the character of individuation and inclusion, which is to say, lacks the characteristics of a multiplicity. This is why the enemy is always one, and all the traits of individuality can be submerged behind the appearance of this opposition. The enemy does not have a particular face (only a general and indiscriminate one), and likewise the enemy does not speak (at least, the expression of an enemy is not individual and its speech is only undifferentiated hatred). The enemy stands for the nothingness in the self and in the world; therefore, in facing the enemy, I only glimpse the force of negation that threatens to reduce the self and the world to the same nothingness.

As we know from the ethical philosophy of Emmanuel Levinas, "the face" is anterior to the self-reflexive identity of the ego with the other, either as the coexistence of two terms in a "logical unity" or as the subject of "transcendental apperception" as in phenomenological intentionality (i.e., "consciousness of"). Therefore, ethical difference can only be phrased in the accusative mode, which is derived from intersubjective space that is primordially asymmetrical; it is only in this manner that it is introduced as not only severely restricting the ego's own freedom and self-presence but also making possible and even provoking the two extreme poles of erotic obsession *(eros)* and destructive violence *(abaddon)*. Accordingly, first, for Levinas it is the very appearance of the face that is not only responsible for provoking violence but also offers the only possibility of peace; second, as radically "unthematizable" (for example, as a generalizable sign of recognition that belongs to humanity), the face is always prone to misrecognition, distortion, and even "perversion" (foregrounding Derrida's observation, which I return to in the next chapter, that any claim of hospitality is "an irreducible pervertibilty").[15] This is because the very form of egoistic recognition always flows from the self to the other, a polarity that cannot be reversed except in the recognition of a form of alterity that cannot be incorporated in the ego's own substance; however, this alterity is perceived as a limit to the ego's own desire for freedom, as a "hostage-situation," and thus incites the primordial urge on the part of the conscious ego to withdraw from the world of others and to close itself up in its own substance.

In both his earlier and the later works, in his analysis of the relationships brought about by *eros* as a "pathos of distance in proximity" where the asymmetrical nature of this duality of beings is maintained, Levinas also locates the primary asymmetrical relationship between the enemy and the friend as determining key political concepts in which the asymmetrical formations belonging to racism and ethnocentrism are determined as well.[16] Consequently, in the same but opposite measure that the failure of communication in love constitutes the alterity of the other as an object of obsession and desire, equally the failure of communication in hostility and warfare constitutes the presence of the stranger qua enemy as the object of impersonal hatred and derision. In both subjective states the other appears as the one who holds me hostage and persecutes me, and in the case of the latter the ego can only hope to escape by fusing its own being with the anonymous and impersonal power of the collective, the group, the nation, the people, or the race. "To this collectivity of comrades," Levinas writes earlier in *De l'existence à l'existant* (1947), "we contrast the I-you collectivity which precedes it. It is not participation in a third term—intermediate person, truth, dogma, work, profession, interest, dwelling, or meal; that is, it is not communion."[17] Thus, paradoxically, the idea of fusion that informs the "we" of collectivity around a common object, a work, or a third term is always in danger of forgetting and potentially betraying the social relation to others, later defined in terms of passivity that is not simply passive, of a vulnerability that is not merely sentimental, and, finally, of a responsibility that is not merely moral. Recalling Deleuze's conceptual persona of a "Socrates who becomes Jewish," we might now define this more explicitly as Levinas's ethical strategy, which takes the form of a radical wager (perhaps even more powerful than Blaise Pascal's wager for the early modern Christian): to install in the very seat of subjectivity, in the heart of the ego, the obligation to the stranger-guest as a fundamental limit to sovereignty of the ego, a limit that is defined in terms of fundamental passivity, obsession, and desire.[18]

Yet in approaching the question of "who is the friend?" is not the seemingly spontaneous recognition of the friend from an infinite number of possible different social relationships an actual instance of a concrete multiplicity? This would depend, however, on the factors that predetermine the possibility of friendship, and we must recognize that this apparent spontaneity is always already limited by a number of prior determinations. In a short philosophical text on the nature of free will, Gottfried Leibniz wrote the following on the limitations of spontaneity and predetermination:

> Although we act with spontaneity, in that there is a principle of action within us, and we are not without life and do not need to be pushed around like puppets, and although our spontaneity is conjoined with knowledge and deliberation or choice, which makes our actions voluntary, nevertheless we must acknowledge that we are always predetermined, and apart from our previous inclinations and dispositions, new impressions from objects also contribute to incline us, and all these inclinations joined together and balanced against contrary inclinations never fail to form a general prevalent inclination. For as we are dependent on the universe, and as we act in it, it must also be the case that we are acted upon. We determine ourselves, and are free insofar as we act, and we are determined by external things and as it were subject to them insofar as we are acted upon. But in one way or another we are always determined on the inside or from the outside, that is to say more inclined to what happens or what will happen than to what will not.[19]

Following the logic in this passage, can we conclude that friendship is predetermined in the same way? In other words, the principle of spontaneity by which we appear to choose friends is already found to be determined "from the inside or from without." Leibniz calls this form of determination an inclination, and I am particularly interested in the last sentence where Leibniz states that we are more inclined to what happens or what will happen than to what will not. This would appear to imply that friendship is a particular form of social habit that already predetermines the concrete situation of recognizing "who is the friend," and we must admit that in the usual experience of friendship, especially intimate ones, there is a constant and often pathetic assertion of homogeneity (i.e., of like attracts like) that is more inclined to what happens than to what will not. (This is also confirmed by Cicero, who observes that friendship is bordered by so many dangers that "the avoiding of them [requires] not only wisdom but also sheer good luck."[20]) From a Leibnizian perspective, therefore, all our friends are predetermined in a manner that also reduces the importance of individuation as a differential factor, since the one who is my friend and the one who will become my friend are, if not the same person, then at least two expressions of the same inclination. Given that such an inclination is both preindividual and unconscious, this is what Deleuze and Guattari define by the term "molecular."

Nevertheless, as discussed above, even this rudimentary form of social differentiation may still be far preferable to the enemy distinction that reduces the social to one form of opposition, since the distinction operated by friendship still produces the concrete situation of multiple affirmations, even though this situation does not result in an absence of conflict *(stásis)*. Perhaps this is because friendship must be understood as a particular kind of social conflict that is usually experienced as its own negation, or to employ Hegel's terminology again, as a kind of self-negated otherness. To put it more starkly, friendship is the concrete social experience of the negation of the self as a unique, isolated, and purely solipsistic existence; friends must ally themselves against the existence of such a self through the production of common experience.

Perhaps this is why in the practice of friendship there is so much discourse on the mutual affirmation of the same tastes, the same opinions,
the same culture; moreover, many occasions are created in order to
afford the opportunity of mutual affirmation: dinner parties, concerts,
outings of various kinds. Friends will go out into the country to enjoy
the landscape together, the first one saying, "isn't that beautiful?" and
the next one repeating, "yes, isn't that beautiful?" This is the conceptual
labor of friendship in creating a homonymy of taste, leading to the specific production of a sphere of culture that defines the association
between friends, which I think is one of the root meanings of *sensus
communis*. Here I believe we have found again the two senses of *stásis*
evoked above in reference to Plato: the kind of conflict that determines
the concept of the friend is the mutual conflict against an otherness
defined as the separate or isolated existence of the self (or what Sartre
defined as the struggle against "the dangerous reef of solipsism".)[21] The
enemy would then be the name of a social existence reduced to its bar-
est abstraction, bereft of all other social relations, as well as all forms of
dependency and for this reason, either condemned to death, to nothingness, or to wandering outside the limits of community, the stranger
determined as the barbarian or the foreigner.

three

Foreigner (Lat. *perigrinus*)

The Rights of men as Citizens of the world in a cosmo-political
system, shall be restricted to conditions of universal Hospitality.

—Immanuel Kant, *Toward Perpetual Peace*

In the following chapters I explore two related conceptual personae of
the stranger: first, the stranger determined as the foreigner, or simply as
a wanderer *(perigrinus)*; and second, the stranger determined as either
a "stranger-enemy" or a "stranger-guest" *(xénos)*. At the same time,
while not all other persons are strangers, all strangers are necessarily
other people; however, today we must ask who can be defined as a
stranger—that is, from what external boundary or frontier does the
stranger first arrive? This is an important question for us to reconsider,
especially when all contemporary territorial boundaries have been
overrun and made permeable and subject to change, and there is neither a distinctly "foreign" place nor a central location, or polis (i.e., *the*
imperial city, *the* capital). Along with the obsolescence of an earlier
territorial conception of geopolitical formations (such as the form of
the nation-state itself), this might be classified among the various signs
of dispersion that have accompanied the processes of globalization—
the multiplication of centers, the permeability of all borders and territories, and the dizzying loss of orientation between an interior dwelling
place, or homeland, and an uninhabited exterior region, or frontier.

It is important to underline that this general disorientation, which is
already figured spatially in the metaphor of globalization itself, has had

important consequences for the juridical and social determination of the stranger as one who arrives from a definite place that is "foreign" and "outside." Recalling our earlier citation from the etymology of Benveniste: "The stranger is one who comes from outside" (Lat. *aduena*), or simply "one who is beyond the limits of community" (Lat. *perigrinus).* Consequently, "there is no 'stranger' as such; within the diversity of these notions, since the stranger is always a particular stranger, as one who originates from a distinct statute."[1] Moreover, following Derrida's recent interrogation of the concepts of "boundary" or "limit-horizon" that are implied by the above definition of the stranger's particular appearance, we might say that the stranger is the manifestation of a social, political— perhaps even anthropological—aporia. In other words, the stranger is another name for the aporia that exists between what Derrida has defined as the insistence of "a universal (although non-natural) structure and a differential (non-natural but cultural) structure."[2]

The different responses exhibited toward the stranger's perspective reveal a strange "double-bind" (Derrida) that can also be found to structure the material sign of cultural difference as such. This is because the determination of cultural difference must always occur in relation to a perspective introduced by a cultural or social stranger who occupies the border position, so to speak, marking the appearance of the distinction between the inside and outside. Therefore, the recognition of cultural difference appears from the perspective of the stranger who apprehends its "otherness" and introduces this perception as either a hermeneutic factor within the group's self-reflection around its own natural belonging to the group or is conceived as the point where the stranger's perspective is excluded and the stranger comes to be determined as the foreigner. In either event, we can conclude that a stranger's perspective must be maintained—even produced, cultivated, and "worked-over," as in the case of dream-work—in a distinct social notion, whether the idea that characterizes the cultural relation to the stranger takes the form of open warfare or deep feelings of gratitude.

For example, cultural narratives are ineluctably drawn toward the position and consciousness of the stranger as if toward the points of contact with their own external and internal (or psychic) borders. Therefore, the stranger is a being who is situated on the border of the group, at the limit of a collective sense of belonging; at the same time, it is the concrete appearance of the stranger that is the occasion for the group's own internal differentiation, including the spectrum and multiple degrees of familiarity and nonfamiliarity, belonging and nonbelonging, with which any *socius* is dynamically composed. As Georg Simmel first observed concerning the history of the European Jews:

> The stranger is no "owner of soil," . . . and although in intimate relations, he may develop charm and significance, as long as he is considered a stranger in the eyes of the other, he is not an "owner of soil"—soil not only in the physical, but also in the figurative sense of a life substance which is fixed, if not a point in space, at least in an ideal point of the social environment.[3]

We can regard the figure of the stranger as representing the hypostasis of the sociological activity that belongs to the mental life of a given historical society. Consequently, Simmel often describes the being of the stranger in terms similar to the Kantian definition of the schema: the condition and symbolic coordination of the spatial relationships that bring phenomena in touch with points that are either virtual or outside its own closed organization. In the Kantian concept, it is this formal operation of the schema, linked with the imagination that opens the bordered spatial organization of phenomena to a duration, that enables the possibility of movement or change.

From the above descriptions, we might also conclude that the consciousness of the stranger produces a certain imaginary function within the mentality of the group. The logic structuring the relation to the social stranger, as well as the logical coordinates of the stranger's formal perspective in a particular *socius,* can be demonstrated by a poetic formula that can be drawn from Simmel's sociological investigation: the stranger is, at the same time, the distancing of what is near and the nearing of what is distant. Because of this mental activity, any distinct stranger that is identified within a given culture would be a reflection of the material relationships that belong to culture alone; therefore, each stranger embodies a singular limit that cannot be crossed out or translated without doing violence to his very appearance. And yet, because of the extreme ambiguity and the fluid nature that belongs to the signification of borders, including the transformation of the absolute partition of life and death into a shared moment of cultural experience and identity, the anthropological and social categories that determine the being of the stranger suffer an inherent ambiguity—especially when the stranger's entire being is grasped and made to manifest the sign of cultural difference. From these observations we may conclude, therefore, that the difference between cultures bears an important relationship to the manifestation of the intra-anthropological partitions according to which a culture treats its own particular strangers.

Nevertheless, if it is also true, according to Benveniste's definition, that "there is no stranger *as such*" and that every stranger is a case of the particular, then there is also no generalizable or ontological expression of "otherness" from which the positive social stranger originates; thus, the philosophical and ethical notions of the "other" only appear from the perspective that reduces (or brackets) the positive contents of the stranger's being. As a result of this "reduction," all the other concrete attributes that might define the person or the individual vanish into an abstract image of the stranger as someone who bears only a few superficial traits of resemblance (a name, a language, sexual and racial characteristics, age, etc.). Of course, a stranger is usually determined from the perspective of a subject who is "at home," who dwells within his or her own familiar and customary limits; consequently, the stranger appears as a being who is "outside" these limits, who is out of place, or whose very relation to place is as yet unknown and thus likely to become a subject of interrogation. At the border crossing or checkpoint, I present my passport to the border police in order to declare that I am legally a stranger, that I come from a definite place of origin, that my encroachment into another territory is only temporary, and that my estrangement is not volatile or likely to lapse into a permanent state. This is because, first of all, I have presented myself or introduced myself in the sense of "*giving myself up.*" At this very moment, my identity is poised between the senses of citizen and deportee. I have turned myself in to the authorities at the border for questioning, implying that I already have accepted and recognized the authority of one who questions me with regard to my legal identity and who will determine the rights accorded to this identity, specifically with regard to my right to travel "beyond the limits of my own community."

This moment of identification—one might even say "interpellation," since in this moment the stranger is "*hailed*" and must submit himself or herself to the rule of the stranger-host—is constantly threatened by ambiguity and the possible lapses that overdetermine it as a performative event. For example, recently when returning to the United States, a Nigerian woman and her children who were in front of me in line were questioned concerning the reason for their entry, the names and addresses of family members in the United States, the number of times she has crossed the border in the last year, the address and vocation of the brother that she visited in Los Angeles four months earlier, why her visit lasted three months, how she paid for travel to the United States, and, since another family member paid for her, who was sponsoring her current trip and what was the source of this money. The woman compliantly answered these questions with an air of familiarity—apparently, she was no stranger to Homeland Security— even though it was obvious that many of the answers to the questions posed to her were already on the computer screen in front of the agent. Nevertheless, it was clear that her rights at this moment were extremely limited, conditioned by positive laws that all refer more to the state's right to secure and police its own borders and to identify everyone who seeks entry, for whatever reason (economic, political, tourist, commercial, personal, or familial). For example, she could not "prefer to remain a stranger" and refuse to answer certain questions or claim certain information as private or personal without subjecting herself to certain peril, including detainment, further interrogation, and the possible denial of entry. It would appear, from this routine example, that the law's right to identification (or recognition) was more or less absolute—an absolute right of the host to identify the stranger as either enemy or guest—while her right to her own identity, including the right to enjoy a certain sovereignty over possessing its attributes or to offer them freely for the purposes of identification or recognition, is conditional on the absolute priority granted to the state's right to identify all strangers at its borders. Given the regularity of media reports of detainees and certain "other strangers" who are held indefinitely "at the step of the territory," it appears that the state has the right, approaching an absolute right, to protect its borders from encroachment by certain kinds of strangers, to identify all who pass through, and to determine the hostile or peaceful nature of the temporary guest.

As another example, while entering Dublin a few years ago as a "traveling professor," a man in front of me was suddenly detained when it was discovered that he had criminal charges pending in another country. He was denied entry; in fact, he was asked to wait outside the gate until officials from Interpol arrived armed with machine guns to take him into custody. An armed guard immediately appeared from a room just to the side of the booth to attend to the man and keep him company while the police were en route. He was a Polish laborer who was entering Dublin to undertake some work, but the information concerning his criminal activity in his own country had caught up with him. It was clear that the state had the right to deny his right as a stranger and foreigner—his identity as a suspected criminal had circumvented his rights as a stranger, a visitor, a guest, a temporary worker—and the state was within its right to rescind the rule of hospitality. From these common examples—I could provide others, including the reports of detainees and certain "other strangers" who are being held indefinitely in prisons outside the United States since 9/11—this right appears unconditional. The state's right to sovereignty over the integrity of its own territory is not determined by mutual consent or recognition; if it were, then this would be a conditional right, contingent on the recognition of this right by another subject. As in the case of the Nigerian woman recounted above, the state's right does not flow from her recognition of its authority; it would exist without her consent, which is why she does not have the right to remain a stranger to it or refuse to become subject to its mandate. Of course, as in the second example, of the man who was refused entry after being identified as a suspected criminal (in other words, as a potential "enemy"), the state can enforce its right, but this is not the source of its sovereignty either, which is to say that the right of territory is not necessarily derived from its force or threat of violence but, recalling the definition given by Benveniste above, appears as something statutory. As Derrida has written concerning this strange tension that is also exhibited in both occasions around the question of hospitality: "This collusion between the violence or the force of law *(Gewalt)* on one side, and hospitality on the other, seems to depend, in an absolutely radical way, on hospitality being inscribed in the form of a right."[4]

In the third definitive article to his treatise *Toward Perpetual Peace,* Kant argues that the stranger's right to hospitality can be understood as a "universal right." He derives the universal nature of this right from two sources: first, from the law of nature *(ius naturale),* which is the universal right to the preservation of one's own nature, which is to say, one's own life; and second (and unique to Kant's theory of right, as I return to discuss in the conclusion), from what could be called the universal right of society *(Gesellschaft)*— that is, "a right of temporary sojourn, a right to associate *(zugessellen),* which all men have."[5] At the same time, the right to hospitality is provisional and temporary (i.e., a right of temporary resort or visitation) for Kant and thus is not to be confused with the right of being determined as a "stranger-guest," as I discuss in the next section. Accordingly, "the stranger may not lay claim to be entertained by right as a guest—for this would require a special friendly compact to make him for a certain time the member of a household—he may only claim a Right of Resort or of visitation."[6] In the Kantian definition, moreover, the right to hospitality can be understood as belonging to the class of rights pertaining to *immunity.* Strangers shall be immune from immediately being treated as an enemy; although "one may refuse to receive him when this can be done without causing his destruction, so long as he peacefully occupies his place, one may not treat him with hostility."[7] Thus, the stranger must not initially be identified as an enemy, nor should the stranger's intention be immediately determined as hostile; such a determination should only come about after the fact, when the stranger violates one of the conditions of hospitality, that of peacefully occupying his place.

We might wonder, however, what is "universal" in this case, and how this right can be understood over and against what appears to be the absolute right of the state. In his article, Kant asserts that, universally, every stranger has a right to expect hospitality; that is to say, according to Kant's definition, "hospitality means the right of a stranger not to be treated as an enemy when he arrives in the land of another."[8] Of course, this in no way guarantees hospitality, since this right can be violated or simply unacknowledged, and the stranger can be just as easily treated with hostility, killed, incarcerated, held hostage, or placed in slavery. As an aside, the United States, post 9/11, has entered a period in which the principle of universal hospitality has been partially suspended and the state engages in an open violation of every stranger's right to hospitality as this was first defined by Kant. Again, according to Kant's original definition, "hospitality means the right of a stranger not to be treated as an enemy when he arrives in the land of another." However, in a period of heightened security, tightening of boundary controls, and even a temporary suspension of hospitality to certain foreigners, one might question if the right to hospitality can exist in view of the United States' claim that it has the right to suspend the presumption of hospitality, or to treat certain strangers (particularly those whose names indicate Arab origin and descent) as "potential enemies." Moreover, the question of rights becomes especially acute where there is no force of law that can resolve the observance of this right, since there is no universal police force that can be present to monitor and, if need be, enforce this right for each and every occasion when a stranger arrives in the land of another. Hospitality is not a law, therefore, and it can only theoretically govern different occasions as an ethical principle in a discourse of rights pertaining to the treatment of strangers. Since *there is no law of hospitality,* we might identify a certain ambiguity concerning the different legal and juridical expressions of hospitality as a right that remains "imperfect and conditional." As Derrida writes, "Since this right, whether private or familial, can only be exercised and guaranteed by the mediation of a public right or a State right, the perversion [of right itself] is unleashed from the inside."[9]

Returning to the assertion of "the right of association" as one of the underlying principles of hospitality, it is important to notice here that Kant's discussion departs significantly from a traditional discourse of rights. Although "association" (or society in general) is universally the condition of the discourse of rights—if there were no society, there would be no need for a discourse that stipulates the conditions and the limits of actions that define the social bond—it also true that "association" is usually not listed as an explicit right, except in the narrower sense of the right to "political association." However, Kant is not speaking here of a right to political association (a right to self-government or self-legislation) but rather of a right to "associate" (a natural right to society) in a more general and even universal sense. That is, he is speaking of the human as an essentially *gregarious* animal, though in a sense not strictly limited to the subject as a political animal *(homo politikoi)* but as an animal that "associates" with others in order *to preserve its essential nature.* In the accompanying phrase, "the right to temporary sojourn," moreover, Kant seems to further define that the primary motive for "association" is not politics but something more akin to travel, commerce, communication, translation—in short, all forms and manners of "intercourse." In other words, the universal right of hospitality pertains to the definition of the human as a stranger, and the stranger is always one who travels, who departs from his or her place in the customary and familiar, who sets out on the open road. But then, if hospitality is a right that naturally belongs to the stranger who travels, then how can the stranger also be defined by Kant as one who "peacefully keeps to his place"? Of course, the irony implicit in Kant's definition is the inherent contradiction it contains, since no stranger qua stranger could ever be said to actually keep to his place, since the stranger is, by definition, one who sets out, who departs from his place and arrives at another.

In the *Introduction to Metaphysics* (1953), Heidegger points to the essential definition of the Greek as "a stranger" but also to the Greek *dasein* as involving the process of "becoming a stranger" of estrangement, which is fundamentally bound to the sense of movement. The stranger in movement, or the movement of estrangement, is both the "casting off from" and "casting out of" *(poeisis)* the limits of place *(poria)*. Heidegger's commentary in the following passage on this proto-European stranger reveals the essential relation to migration:

> We are taking the strange, the uncanny (*Das Unheimliche),* as that which casts us out of the homely, i.e., the customary, the familiar, or the secure. The "unhomely" prevents us from making ourselves at home and therein it is overpowering. Man is the strangest of all, not only because he passes his life amid the strange understood in this sense, but because he departs [he sets out and travels] from his customary, familiar limits, because he is the violent one, who, tending toward the strange in the sense of the overpowering, surpasses the limit of the familiar.[10]

From the above passage we might conclude that, in a certain sense, it is a natural state for man to be in motion—that is, to enter into a state that necessarily entails becoming a stranger. For Kant, however, the implicit aim of the process of estrangement and movement is nothing other than society itself, but society no longer determined by political goals or the familial and ethnic kinship; rather, the goal is society itself determined as visitation, temporary association, communication, *commercium,* and the exchange of the guest–host relationship. At the same time, it is important to emphasize that the universal right to society *(Gesellschaft)* is not entirely a positive state in Kant's account either but first arrives from the fact that humans cannot disperse themselves across the continuous and limited surface of the globe to avoid each other and eventually must "finally tolerate the presence of one another."[11] According to this description, the "right to associate" does not practically originate from a positive and gregarious spirit but rather is something that only gradually develops in man, begrudgingly, as a spirit of toleration—in other words, in the expression of the personality of the law itself. This is because, left to our own inclinations, we would prefer to be alone, not disturbed or agitated by the irritating presence of others. Implicitly, it is this impulse that functions as the cause of the initial dispersion of individuals and communities in Kant's description of nature's "grand design" in which each attempts to find, to quote a biblical phrase that is frequently employed by Levinas, "his own place in the sun." Consequently, there is a constant and overriding drive to withdraw from proximity to others and, one might easily imagine, especially from strangers whose very presence brings an "allergic reaction" on the part of the ego, since every encounter with a stranger brings with it the inevitable specter of hostility. Yet since this withdrawal has become practically impossible, when translated onto the confines of the earth's inhabitable surface (basically, the limited number of hospitable regions interspersed by vast wastelands of water, sand, and ice), we must inevitably learn to put up with the presence of others and, according to Kant, even the most annoying of others, with the presence of strangers to whom we owe a certain debt of hospitality.

It goes without saying, of course, that both tolerance and hospitality are inherently conditional by their very definition. There is a limit to my hospitality, beyond which I can refuse any further hospitality to the guest who attempts to usurp my place (or, to employ Kant's phrase again, who "doesn't peacefully keep to his place"). Likewise, I can only be tolerant of the other's presence up to a certain point, after which I am fully within my rights to refuse my own presence in retaliation, which is to say, a threat to withdraw any further society. Both of these conditions, which are common enough to be part of any social relation and comprise the implicit understanding of the conditions and external limits of the most quotidian of social liaisons, have the possibility of open hostility as their ultimate guarantee. Within these limits, there is society defined as the possibility of hospitality, exchange, communication, and generosity. Beyond them, there is only the promise of aggression, war, retaliation, and even genocide. Consequently, Kant's use of the word "tolerance" *(Duldsamkeit)* to characterize what could be called the fundamental mood of society *(Gesellschaft)* is extremely appropriate, since tolerance *(Duldung)* is merely the "negative" (i.e., absence) of open aggression, or warfare. If Kant seems to designate this as the dominant social spirit, perhaps this is utterly practical, since it perfectly describes the feeling we have toward others we encounter—especially toward others who appear to us as strangers and for whom we have no previous social relationship, except the most abstract relation that defines the spirit of law itself, which only minimally demands of us simply to be *tolerant of the other's bare right to exist.*

What Kant is describing in very subtle terms can be developed in a manner that is not very different from the description of the social relation to another person as a certain "hostage-taking" situation in the writings of Levinas.[12] As with Kant, perhaps to an even more emphatic degree, Levinas describes the personality of the ego by the natural qualities of solipsism and narcissism and the interruption of society as an unwelcome intrusion into this primitive state of nature (i.e., think of the infant who is not aware that others exist outside the confines of his or her primitive consciousness, including the parents and other global persons). Therefore, we might even consider the being of the stranger as a *hypostasis* of this intrusive encounter with society, in the sense that every appearance of the stranger is accompanied by a law that demands the subject be hospitable and tolerate the irritating presence of another, which the solipsistic ego would naturally understand as a law of being hostage to the presence of the stranger. Naturally, such a law cannot but create a degree of resentment—both to the stranger and to the social ideas of toleration and hospitality. This resentment forms the character of the "social egoism" that marks the inherent limits of any expression of toleration and hospitality.

Recalling the examples offered earlier, we could hypothesize that certain communities, such as the state and its representatives, have incarnated a certain portion of this spirit of resentment and social egoism. This often colors what could be called the fundamental personality of certain groups and associations, even to a degree that certain subjective expressions of this personality are translated to the individual members who identify with the group's overall conservative interests. Why is it, I have often wondered, that the border officials never seem entirely happy to greet me when I visit another country? Why do they respond to my simple request for hospitality with a subtle look of menace in their eyes? If this seems somewhat "Kafkaesque," perhaps it is because the answer to the above queries can be found in the short parable related to Josef K. at the end of *The Trial,* in which it is said that the law is neither particularly happy to see you come nor very sad to see you go. It merely allows you to enter or gives you permission to depart with an equal amount of indifference. Its affect, therefore, is purely a lack of emotion, that of tolerating you in principle but only under certain conditions and never with any display of interest or affection. In this sense, in the eyes of the law, we are all strangers; although this does not necessarily presuppose that all strangers are equal in the eyes of the law.

At this point in our analysis, therefore, we should note one flaw in Kant's definition of the stranger's universal right of hospitality—that it presupposes that every stranger is potentially a host, or that he or she has a commensurable and reciprocal position vis-à-vis the master in his own land. From its origins in the Greek systems of philosophy and civil law (the laws of the polis), we might conclude that the concept of the stranger we have been discussing is that of a very particular stranger indeed! The European stranger is essentially a despot (master of the house), and must therefore be capable both of travel and of returning to his own home. In other words, the "universal right of hospitality" is a right that only exists between equals; the host merely recognizes himself in the place of the guest, "respects" his own law and enjoys his own substance in temporarily "alienating" his own mastery to the guest, who appears in the place of the master. The host welcomes the guest, who, in turn, recognizes the host as host, the master as master. It is for this reason, as Derrida argues elsewhere, that the identity of the master is in some sense completely dependent on the relation to the guest and the stranger: "It gives the welcoming host the possibility of having access to his own proper place."[13] The concept of right in the so-called right to hospitality, consequently, must be understood specifically in the form of an alienated right—the right of the master, or host, which has undergone alienation in the place of the guest. It is this form of alienation that gives all acts of hospitality a certain exchange character, and the German language that Kant employed uniquely offers the resources for distinguishing between alienation defined as "estrangement" *(entfremden)* and alienation defined as "exchange" *(eintäuschen)*. But this also implies that the stranger is merely an alienated master, and the stranger's right to hospitality, then, only extends to those subjects who can change positions in the reciprocity of the guest–host relationship, or who can temporarily alienate their status as masters in one place in order to enjoy the temporary sojourn as the guest in another.

If hospitality only pertains to the rights of strangers and strangers are implicitly defined as displaced masters or hosts who enter into a pact or exchange with other hosts, then how does the right to hospitality extend to those who cannot claim this right? In the case of the particular stranger defined as the "deportee," for example, as we will see later on, or in the case of the stranger who appears as the homeless refugee within the national borders of the state, the mutual recognition between hosts is not a basis for the claim to hospitality, which is why it may often go unrecognized in their case. In other words, if we have discovered earlier that the right of every stranger to temporary sojourn is based on a more fundamental right, "the right to society," we might notice in the exceptional case of these strangers that this right to association remains a source of ambiguity, and this is especially true on those occasions where violence, either natural or in the case of wars, is located as the cause of estrangement. Thus, when the desire for association (or society) is not the motive of the stranger's movement, we might wonder whether there is a right to hospitality, properly speaking. The "refugee," for example, whose very existence petitions a host for refuge, for safety and protection, is neither a guest nor another host; therefore, the refugee is not a stranger in the sense defined above and thus, as we might expect, has no legal claim to hospitality. There is no pact that the refugee can claim, no exchange of hospitality, but rather a purely dependent and statutory relationship to the host. In this case, it is often only in the name of another master, or a "third" (in the name of justice or human rights), that intervenes to demand hospitality for the other who cannot claim this right for himself or herself. In other words, it is only in the name of another despot, perhaps even a "universal despot" (humanity), that the law of hospitality is extended to give temporary sojourn to the stateless and the homeless.

This is the legal character and personality of the claim for "respect and dignity" (*aidós,* a specific obligation I discuss in the next chapter), which is that of a surrogate claim, in the name of another host. However, because this claim is not made as a pact among equals, a certain ambiguity surrounds it, and what is granted is not hospitality strictly speaking but merely the minimal recognition of the right to live (i.e., to the juridical status "bare life," employing Agamben's phrasing). Consequently, in the refugee camps that exist under this contract between two hosts, only a minimal degree of hospitality is guaranteed, barely enough to preserve the image of humanity from injury—that is, nothing more than to preserve the image of the host from suffering violence and degradation (recalling Plato's image of "self-laceration" in reference to the image of the body proper of the host). As Jacques Lacan first argued, acts of charity are not necessarily "altruistic" in nature but are inevitably invested with a certain narcissistic spirit of self-preservation—most of all, the investment in the proper image of the human body as whole and intact. Consequently, because there is a certain ambiguity that also defines the body as a "host," we may notice that the care extended to refugees is often limited to the preservation of the body and does not address the particularity of the individuals or their rights, which go unrecognized as a class. Although the refugee is also a subject who has suffered the violation of his or her political, legal, and juridical rights as well, it is primarily to the body that a certain debt of hospitality is paid in the name of the master-host. In other words, the refugee, as a certain limit-example of the stranger, has been reduced to a purely bodily existence and exists only to the degree that the violence suffered by the body causes the host to suffer through sympathy and to feed, clothe, and nourish the body of the refugee defined as an unwelcome and temporary guest.

Earlier on I cited a passage by Derrida in which he locates the degradation of the stranger's right to hospitality at the interior of the private and familial space of intimacy. In other words, according to Derrida, all perversion begins at home, but perversion of what, exactly? Or rather, how is the stranger's right to hospitality perverted by the primitive formations of interest and power (and desire) that flow from these intimate and familial spaces? These spaces have traditionally been defined according to the exclusive sense of the master (of the host and despot), in which the stranger has no place. In the sphere of the family, the stranger is first recognized as absolutely strange or foreign, or as not belonging and, therefore, as having no place from which to appeal in the name of rights. Recalling a familiar scene from a play by Bertolt Brecht in which a stranger suddenly enters the kitchen of a family dwelling, prompting the shock and fear on the part of the members of the family and the father's violent response, every incursion of the stranger into the home is perceived as an act of violence, and thus, the stranger is immediately greeted there as an enemy. If there is no stranger in the sphere of the home, then we might conclude that there is no hospitality either, and no possibility of any discourse of rights, unless this is first introduced or mediated by some public law or civic right that is also accorded to members of the familial bond as surrogate rights, as in the claims of the right to immunity from violence in laws prohibiting child and spousal abuse. We might even phrase this in a more extreme sense by saying that the stranger has no relation to those spaces defined predominately by intimacy or familial belonging, and this is confirmed by the subjective mood that characterizes our relation to strangers as distinctly lacking these qualities.[14] Hence, the subjective and emotional qualities that define our relation to strangers are bereft of any attributes of intimacy; in fact, they are characterized by the opposite affects—by a coolness of detachment, a certain indifference with regard to the person of the stranger, and even a certain sense of hostility or enmity toward the stranger's presence. These emotional qualities that so naturally characterize our relation to strangers are not arbitrary but originate from the statutes that determine the stranger's "place in society" at the boundary of the association (or "pact") of the so-called natural bond—of kinship, blood (or race), intimate or private ties of affection, and desire.

One can see why Derrida would determine these intimate spheres as the origin of potential perversion of the rights accorded to strangers, since the stranger has no place there but is constitutionally defined as being outside or beyond these pacts (of kinship, blood or race, linguistic community, and even the quasi-contractual bonds of friendship and sexual intimacy). Consequently, as Derrida writes, "there is no foreigner [*xénos,* actually referring to the "guest stranger" as I discuss next] before or outside the *xénia,* this pact or exchange with a group, or more precisely, this line of descent."[15] In other words, recalling the definition given by Benveniste above, if there is no stranger that does not originate from a distinct statute or law, then the specific statute in question is the one that first constitutes the "pact" or "exchange" between members of a group, particularly the exchange and lawful transmission of identity and territory through a line of descent. The family member, or the one whose identity is constituted by the pact of the family, can enter the home without first asking permission, since this is already a stipulated term of the right to "association" that belongs to those subjects located at the interior of *domus.* However, as one who first approaches from outside the limits of the natural community, the stranger has no right to claim the provisions of this original social bond. From this analysis, therefore, it seems that the stranger's right to hospitality is immanently open to perversion from the fact that this very right can only be defined in relation to the law of the host. As Derrida writes:

> To suppose that one could have a perfectly stabilized concept of hospitality, something I do not believe, is the moment when it is already in the process of being perverted. The passage from pure hospitality to right and to politics is one of perversion, inasmuch as the condition [of

perversion] is already implicit in this passage and, as a consequence, so is the call to a certain perfectability [of hospitality], to the necessity of ameliorating without end, indefinitely, its determinations, conditions, legislative definitions whether familial, local, national, or international . . . . Hospitality is, thus, immediately pervertible and perfectible at once: there is no ideal hospitality, but only statutes that are always already in the process of being perverted and of being ameliorated, even though such amelioration carries with itself the seeds of all future perversions.[16]

Let us return to the Kantian notion of "universal hospitality" in order to again raise the question concerning the origin of the stranger's right to hospitality and how this can be understood against the group's right to assign the terms (or statutes) that determine the very identity of the stranger *as if from the inside.* As Kant argues, the stranger's right to lay claim to the surface of the earth stems from an original state in which "no one had more right than another to a particular part of the earth."[17] As the earth became more peopled and territories were established, particular rights were recognized by treaty and colonization. However, according to Kant, it is the design of the great artist, nature *(natura daedala rerum),* to populate the entire globe and utilize war as an instrument to distribute populations equally across its surface, even to the most uninhabitable and desolate regions of the earth (deserts, oceans, vast frozen steppes, and inaccessible jungles). In his argument, Kant resorts to a speculative myth concerning an original and even primordial time when no one enjoyed the right to lay claim to any part of the earth, since everyone possessed the surface of the earth equally. Thus the origin of both the stranger's right to demand hospitality and the right to associate through travel and visitation (a right that "all men have") have their origins in the "common possession of the surface of the earth."[18]

In its most obvious sense, of course, this original state can be defined temporally, referring to a time before the invention of "territory," before the families and clans claimed homes and tribal plots or principalities

and nations emerged to claim certain whole portions of the earth's surface, which they determined to solely possess and to enjoy exclusive
rights to as their own native soil. However, Kant also asserts that this
original determination continues to define the "uninhabitable parts of
the earth," such as the seas and deserts (and today one could also add
the air to Kant's list of vast wastelands that lie between communities).
Thus, the common possession of the earth also extends to define these
spaces that no one can exclusively possess but that are defined as spaces
of pure communication or translation, which today would especially
describe the wasteland of virtual spaces and the networked communications of satellites and internetworked communications. Since these
spaces cannot be inhabited, the notion of "territory" cannot be applied
to them; moreover, because the mutual interests to protect these spaces
invest them, they are defined primarily by international laws that stipu-
late their temporary possession as the open spaces that lie between and
outside the boundaries of the home. Consequently, the laws that define
the guest–host relationship would not extend to these spaces either,
since there are no masters, and therefore no hosts, and everyone is
equally a stranger in these uninhabitable regions of the earth. It is precisely here, as Kant argues, where there is neither guest nor host, master
nor stranger (neither foreigner nor stranger-guest), that the idea "of a
law of world citizenship is no high-flown or exaggerated notion . . . but
rather a supplement to the unwritten law of the civil and international
law, indispensable for the maintenance of the public human rights and
hence also of perpetual peace."[19]

What is the unwritten law that Kant speaks of here but the one that
we also found at the basis of the stranger's right to hospitality and right
to association (or society) and communication (linguistically, but also
through travel and commercial intercourse)? The precedence—even
transcendence—of this unwritten law can easily be demonstrated by the
fact that, despite its absolute claim to sovereignty over its own borders
and the right to enforce this claim by threats of violence or power (or
by the constant vigilance of its border police), all borders nevertheless
remain indefinitely open to communication with what lies outside, to

the inevitable intercourse with strangers and foreigners (even before these are determined as "guests" or "enemies"). Here, we might pause to reflect that one of the underlying principles of globalization has been the sheer increase of communications of all kinds, particularly the rapid and almost instantaneous forms of intercourse such as television, faxes, the Internet, and cellular and satellite transmissions. These forms of communication can also be defined as pure spaces of communication and translation between communities governed by pacts and legal obligations and thus as subject to international and civil laws that pertain to spaces outside the territorial sovereignties that determine the guest–host relationship. Thus, it has almost become a cliché to say that globalization has also been marked by the quantitative increase of such spaces, but what is important to underscore is the growing frequency of the encounters where there is neither guest nor master (no "stranger-host" relationship), encounters that exist outside or even before the question of hospitality, since they take place outside the laws that continue to define the boundaries of the territory, even though they often occur inside the very limits of the proper domain, native soil, or home. In other words, we might see this phenomenon as the materialization of Kant's thesis concerning the unwritten law of association—that is, the new forms of society that are emerging as a result of the communication between *particular strangers,* for whom the statutes concerning the positive limits of legal obligation and the stranger's right to hospitality are still in the process of being written today.

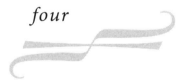

four

Stranger (Gr. *xénos*)

We must learn again to read Homer.

—Émile Benveniste, *Le Vocabulaire des institutions Indo-Européennes*

Following the discussion of the foreigner as the "stranger-wanderer" (or immigrant), it would seem that the concept of the foreigner as the "stranger-guest" *(xénos)* would naturally be a hybrid of these two social relationships in contradistinction to the determination of the friend *(phílos)*. However, nothing could be further from the truth, and there has been a confusion of the two terms over time; therefore, it is around the particular social form of the stranger-guest that we will need to return again to the rich analysis of Benveniste. Our earlier analysis of the Latin term *perigrinus* pertained to the stranger determined as a wanderer or immigrant, and we began by reflecting on the quantitative increase of such strangers as the result of globalization and the multiple encounters that occur today outside the earlier boundaries of the Roman *Imperium*. However, there is another kind of stranger that appears in Benveniste's analysis of the fundamental Indo-European institutions and pertains to the stranger determined as the stranger-guest *(xénos)* —that is, at the very boundary of the stranger–guest and stranger–enemy distinction. It is this form, according to Benveniste, that explicitly belongs to the primitive institution of friendship *(philótēs)*.

In one sense, the term *phílos* demarcates the social sphere of those members "who directly have a share in political rights" *(co-partageant des droits politiques),* thus linking the interior of the family to the interior boundaries of the city. All who are found to dwell inside this boundary are linked together by a circle of friendship, which is strictly determined as a form of political dependency that takes its original condition from the family or natural community. However, prior to designating any sentimentality or affective meaning that often colors the concept of friendship today, the original significance establishes the direct relationship even topologically considered, between the house, the enclosure of the family, and the enclosure of the city where the citizen is found to dwell. As Benveniste argues, "These are the three progressive steps that lead directly from the group to the city."[1]

> From the ancient relationship of "friendship," which Vedic *śeva-* denotes, to the better attested sense "group by matrimonial alliance," which appears in Germanic *heiwa-* and, finally, to the concept of "co-partners in political rights," which Latin *cīvis* expresses, there is a progression in three stages from the "closed group" to "the city."[2]

According to this metaphoric progression across different steps, or thresholds, that belong to the polis, the minute the familial subject crosses the threshold of the home he or she may be outside the closed group of the family but still exists within the circle of the polis that determines his or her social identity as a citizen, which is then linked dialectically to his or her identity as a member of the family, as if allowing the subject to traverse from one formal identity to the next, thereby creating a visible and tangible boundary between inside and outside. At the same time, however, the very boundary between the home and the polis is effectively crossed through or canceled out so that these two social identities appear as simply a natural extension of the same civil right, implying a community of habitat and political rights. This constitutes an anomaly from which the abstract notion of "citizenship" is derived, which Benveniste argues is "peculiar" to the Latin vocabulary.[3]

At the same time, it goes without saying that there are also other social beings found to be present, occasionally, both in the home and in the streets of the city, but who do not share the same political right of hospitality. These are called the stranger-guests, or foreigners *(xénoi)*. Given that their point of entry into the center of the city is not from the space of the home but from "outside" (again, "the stranger is one who arrives from outside"), they do not belong to the progressive determination of *phílos* but constitute an exception to this social form of identity and the sentiments normally associated with members of a closed group. The appearance of the stranger-guest also marks a transformed sentimentality, however, as Benveniste argues, one that is strictly determined by a restricted and special meaning of *philótēs* as the bond of obligation or exchange that occurs only artificially by means of a special pact or contract that is originally sealed by a "kiss" *(phílēma)*, which originally had no affective meaning, being rather a pure symbol of recognition that belongs to the ritual of hospitality.[4] As Benveniste recounts, a second symbol assumes the form of a broken ring, the two halves of which are exchanged between host and guest as a symbol of the pact of the relationship. The fact that both these symbols have evolved and now belong to the modern (Christian) institution of marriage gives us the precise sense of the distance, as well as a genealogical affiliation, between these two original forms of social obligation, or "hostage-taking."[5]

At this point, however, Benveniste argues that the possessive form of the stranger–friend relationship indicates the obligatory comportment of the host to the guest and is not reducible to a simple linguistic possessive. As he writes:

> We are arrested by the well-known fact that in Homer *phílos* has two senses: first of all the one of friend, *phílos* does not designate the value of friendship, but rather possession. . . . It is a mark of possession that expresses no amicable relation. Therefore, in its purely social signification, as in other Indo-European languages, "my friend" would bear no particular sentimental association, except the nomination of familial or juridical possession as in "my spouse," or "my child."[6]

And yet, if the possessive form of "my guest" would at some point become equivalent to "my spouse," then this only occurs linguistically following the transposition of the original concept's signification outside the ritual institution of hospitality, as a result of which its original social meaning is hopelessly lost. In other words, here Benveniste perceives that the reduction of *phílos* to a simple possessive ("my friend," like "my spouse," even extending to "myself" or "my kind") could entail the loss of the original institutional and ritual determination of the social idea of friendship as the expression of behavior that is incumbent on a member of the community toward a *xénos*, a "stranger-guest."[7] That is to say, reduced to its linguistic and grammatical sense, its original social meaning becomes abstract. Like a coin worn from being passed from hand to hand, therefore, the archaic ritual conventions of the *philótēs* have been lost, perhaps irretrievably so. Thus, the most remarkable moment of Benveniste's long and complex analysis of the meaning of the Greek *phílos* and the French *ami* occurs when he radically separates the simple grammatical sense of the possessive from any affective meaning ascribed to its adjective. In this sense *phílos* designates a possessive sense—"my friend"—and contains no affective or sentimental meaning at this point; moreover, as a possessive, *phílos* can only be expressed by the host to designate possession and a formal obligation associated with dependency or political alliance, such as in the common phrase "friend of Caesar," or later, "friend of Christ."

At this point, let us return to ask in what manner the Greek language dreams of a purely sentimental value of "friendship" *(philótēs, philía)*. As with the Freudian dream-work, the friend assumes many other latent significations without any regard to their overt semantic content but become pure floating signifiers as in the dream-work itself. Therefore, in a quite dense and remarkably rich section of his own etymological analysis of *phílos*, Benveniste attempts to construct the chain of signifiers that belong to the concept in the manner of an original condensation of poetic metaphors that ultimately serve to displace its original signification. Furthermore, the association to the Freudian dream-work is not arbitrary or accidental, since at one point he determines the destination of the original concept's signification as "repressed." The condensation of signifiers include the following, all of which are derived from the text of Homer, which constitutes a privileged urtext for Benveniste.

First, as I have already referred to above, *phílos* is associated with the act of kissing *(phileîn)* that originally serves as the symbol of mutual recognition that seals the pact between *phíloi*. Thus, according to Herodotus, when Persians greet one another in their travels, in place of exchanging words they kiss one another on the mouth according to a custom that continues to the present day; if there is a difference in social status or hierarchy between the two parties, the kiss is exchanged on the cheek.[8] Once again, Benveniste qualifies this symbol to argue that it initially has no affective or sentimental meaning outside the highly ritualized and symbolic performance of recognition. (However, it is significant that the mouth is the part of the body that is chosen, signifying an act that can only be performed mutually and spontaneously by two separate beings, indicating its fundamental sense of reciprocity—since no one can kiss their own mouth—and thus the choice is logical in addition to being poetic.) Secondly, *phílos* acquires an additional affective value in being associated with the members of the home as the friend who enters the home is greeted in a manner comparable to the spouse with the exchange of gifts that belong to one's own body or private and household economy *(oikos)*.

Throughout his explication of the original social institution of the *philótēs*, Benveniste takes great pain to demonstrate that the origin of the affective nature of the sentiment that belongs to the meaning of the friend today is a figurative outgrowth of one of the earliest Indo-European institutions, that of hospitality between those who are nominated as "friends" *(philótēs)* and that would include both members of the family as well as citizens. In other words, the affective quality that currently belongs to the term, and which has belonged to it for several centuries, since it is present in Cicero as well, marks the transposition of the sentiment of the community into an affective term of the "friend" *(ami)*. In other words, the affective meaning now belonging to the term in most contemporary languages indicates a purely metaphorical (i.e., impure) transposition of the social significance, one that obscures the obligatory and ritual meanings of the act of "hospitization," here employing the neologism that Benveniste coins to refer to the specific social occasions and situations from which the nomination of the friend first appears as a living category, or what I have called, following Deleuze, a conceptual persona.

However, let us also recall at this point Deleuze's assertion that the Greek notion of the "friend" is too complicated and remote, even already from its later Platonic sources, to designate any "living category" in its contemporary sense. Benveniste's own argument seems to confirm this claim; although, the same conclusion is arrived at by a different method of etymological investigation. He concludes:

> All this wealth of concepts was smothered and lost to view once *phílos* was reduced to a vague notion of friendship or wrongly interpreted as a possessive adjective. . . . *As to the etymology of* phílos, *it is now clear that nothing that has been proposed on this subject holds good any longer.*[9]

Here, as elsewhere in the argument concerning other Greek terms that have lost their original semantic and social meaning through the process of translation into the Roman imperial Latin, the implicit aim of Benveniste's entire analysis is that the common and even "banal" meaning of friendship that finds its usage in most contemporary Indo-European languages finds its origin precisely in the Greek language and, specifically, that even the Platonic transformation of the concept radically departed from its Homeric sources. (Hence Benveniste's statement, "It is high time we learned again how to read Homer."[10]) Nevertheless, it would not be accurate to say that Plato was entirely responsible for this metaphorical transformation of the social notion into a simple affective term but rather that it is "the Greek language itself that dreams of according this term an exclusively sentimental value that cannot be derived from its initial social notions."[11] What is remarkable here is the statement that the Greek language is capable of dreaming in sentimental terms and that this "dream" may have infected and contaminated the original social notion of the friend, and by extension, the specific form of dependency and obligation that originally defines the friend as a social entity. As he goes on to defend his privilege of the Homeric usage, Benveniste argues the following:

> In order to understand this complex history, it is important to recall that in Homer the entire vocabulary of moral terms is impregnated with non-individual and purely relational values. What we take as a psychological, affective, and moral terminology, in reality, only indicates the relations of the individual with the members of the group; and the direct connection between certain of these moral terms is appropriately clarified by their initial significations. Thus, there is a constant and direct link in Homer between *phílos* and the concept of *aidós,* a very interesting term that will have to be explored.[12]

As an experiment (and to follow Benveniste's argument), at this point let us perform a radical bracketing of any affective or sentimental sense in defining the concept of the friend, similar to the phenomenological method. Why? First of all, this emotion is a dream that is originally invented by the poetics of the Greek language and not from the concrete social and ritual significations from which the term is derived, as in the case of many other Greek concepts; therefore, it must be radically extirpated in order to arrive at its primitive social notion. In this regard, even many of the contemporary philosophical analyses of hospitality, such as those by Derrida and Levinas, remain far too metaphorical in their translation of the original conceptual personae of the Greek stranger-guest and even the concept of hospitality itself. Even while each philosopher attempts to recover an earlier and even archaic institution of *xénia,* the "stranger–guest" relation that belongs to the institution of hospitality, as if to revive a primitive signification as the philosophical basis for erecting a moral and ethical sensibility toward "the other," both philosophers also attest to the implicit failure of this project, which is primarily owed to two later deformations of the terms themselves in their subsequent translations into Latin and French: first, by a Roman and juridical translation of the *alter huic*; and second, by a scholastic and essentially pseudo-Platonic concept of *autrui.* For example, if I have not employed this term in this study, preferring the more concrete conceptual personae instead, this is because I find the concept of *autrui* still too metaphorical, along with being poetically overdetermined by the sentiments of a pseudo-Christian "piety," to recover some of the original social significations that, according to Benveniste, belonged to the relationship between the host and the stranger-guest. It is also for this reason that throughout this study—but especially in this chapter—I have included the Greek and Latin terms in brackets, along with their diacritical characters, as if to identify "false friends" and restore their identity as "foreign words."

However, at this point we must ask: what would be the archaic basis for the *hospitization of the stranger-guest* in the first place, which is not simply an ethical sense of duty or obligation in the Kantian sense? "It is necessary," Benveniste writes, "in order to fully understand the situation, to represent the *xénos,* of a "guest," who is visiting another country where, as a stranger, he is deprived of all rights, of any protection, as well as any means of existing on his own."[13] It is only in such a limit-situation, however, that the full meaning of the obligation of hospitality appears, according to which the "stranger-guest" is bound to the same observance of community already enjoyed by the natural citizen but by means of a special pact that is premised on the sign of recognition of absolute dependency on the host. As Benveniste writes:

> He finds no other guarantee of protection, therefore, than the one that is accorded to him in the relationship of friendship *(philótēs)*. It is from such an extreme situation that the bond of friendship finds a more restricted and special determination, but as also with the meaning of *phílos* that emerges progressively from the family, both senses originate from a state of absolute dependency (and possession), which then is transposed onto other emotional qualities. What are the emotional qualities? Regard, pity, comfort, respect for the misfortunate; also, honor, loyalty, collective goodwill *(charitas),* and finally "modesty" and "despair."[14]

"Regard, pity, comfort, respect for the misfortunate"—first of all, these are the ethical prescriptions of superiors toward those who are inferior in rank and status; likewise, "honor, loyalty, and collective goodwill" are the affective terms that define the superior's ethical response and responsibility. However, "modesty" and "despair" are the extreme opposites that stand at the absolute limits of all community, since the exhibition of despair cannot be tolerated and must be treated with the virtues of modesty and charity (e.g., to feed the hungry, to clothe the poor). Therefore, these extreme states invoke the community's emotions that define the obligatory behavior toward the host—that is, the ritual observance of hospitality in response to the call for respect, or reverence *(aidôs)*.

As discussed earlier in relation to the foreigner *(perigrinus)*, Derrida has written extensively on precisely this "restricted and special" usage of the term *philótês* to address both a complete state of dependency and an absolute obligation to hospitality (Benveniste's hospitization, or Levinas's "hostage situation"), a responsibility that in a certain sense he has also shown to be a reversal of the superiority embodied by the original institution of the host (as despot, or master), but this might be an arbitrary determination of the real social relationships that have evolved out of this early institution. Just as the friend indicates the sentiment of community that flows out to all of the natural members who already have a share *(partager)* in the political rights of the group (through kinship or inheritance), the affection of friendship directed by the host toward the stranger-guest indicates the emotional qualities that define the special bond of the *philótês*. As one result, the history of this original institution of friendship toward the stranger-guest is remarked by all the failures of this circle of the closed group to complete itself and become absolute—that is, to encompass all the living relationships that belong to the polis.

And yet, it should not go unobserved that what is even more remarkable is the very existence of this special pact or social institution pertaining to the right of the stranger-guest in the first place. This special pact becomes the precedent of the stranger's universal right of hospitality that Kant would later on define as the basis for international law: the "special pacts" or positive customs that are accorded to strangers who travel outside the limits of their own territory, which bind the prospective hosts to certain obligations and duties—first of all, that the stranger not initially be treated as an enemy as long as "he conducts himself peacefully in the place where he happens to be."[15] And yet, the question I have already raised is, what could be the foundation of this so-called universal right of hospitality, which can be called neither universal nor a right in the strictest sense, nor even a duty or obligation in the moral sense, which is dependent upon culture and religion? In this respect, the natural origin of this right presents us with the same mystery as the "Rights of Man," except in this case, we discover the right of hospitality pertains only to a special case of immunity that is restricted to the social being of strangers. In what way can this right be called universal—unless, that is, all people are strangers by nature? Therefore, are there not also strangers who also appear in the very center of the closed group? For example, let us imagine the situation that Benveniste defined above: *at the very center of the city (if not in the very home) appears the existence of a social being who is deprived of all political rights, all protection, and thus any means of existence, which is to say, in a state of absolute dependency on an original host.* Here we discover in the appearance of this being—including the suddenness and the unexpected nature of his or her appearance—a natural corollary to the infant who appears inside the home at the center of the circle of the family. Thus, perhaps the infant is the first and most primitive figure of the stranger-guest, the first appearance of a being who is deprived of all political rights, in a primitive state of absolute dependency, whose very claim to protection or "immunity" is only a surrogate of the host's respect and reverence for this "particular stranger" who appears at the very center of the closed group but whose identity also originates from positive law, custom, and culture.

Following this association of the stranger-guest relation that is also internal to the group, let us recall again the affective and emotional qualities of reverence and respect that belong to the situation involving hospitization in response to the obligation of *aidṓs*. Again, these subjective attitudes first appear from the perspective of a superior host in response to a state of dependency and function as the motives for the overt actions of ritual obligation of friendship, or hospitality. Moreover, as Benveniste shows, it is in the inner sphere of the family that the emotional qualities of reverence, or respect, begin to exclusively define the position of the *oikodespótēs* (the head of the family), also for whom the power of *aidṓs* is solely reserved, especially "pity" for those who are completely dependent on his sovereignty. To this subjective quality we find other emotions that belong naturally to the members of the household group and that constitute a state of mutual dependency and obligation between master and host, such as regard, comfort, honor, loyalty, goodwill *(charitas),* and, finally, "modesty" and "despair." The sexual relation in particular is reserved for the feelings of modesty and restraint, particularly toward women and children; honor, loyalty, and collective goodwill appear to generally characterize all the subjective relations between members of the household; and, finally, the extreme sentiments of "pity" and "despair" do not seem to be tolerated and demand immediate hospitization by the *oikodespótēs*. The question of how these emotional qualities first appear to naturally determine the relationships of this group is perhaps unanswerable, but what is more important is that these subjective comportments begin to objectively define the special nature of the social relationships that one finds there.

According to Benveniste, what is most crucial to observe is that many of these same emotional qualities are transported outside the closed circle of the group in order to reappear in the institution of the *philótēs,* but again, only by means of a "special pact." However, in the Roman and Christian worlds that follow, it is the area of religion *(religio)* that is gradually reserved for this "restricted and special pact," as well as many of the subjective comportments between members of a natural community and a host of strangers. However, what is more significant is that it is also around this special pact that one finds the extreme expressions of pity and despair that now determine the state of absolute dependency of the creature before his God and, in response, a special kind of reverence and obligation that is particularly reserved for the relation between God, the "Host of hosts" (that is, the absolute *oikodespótēs*), and his own particular stranger-guests. Christianity, in its most primitive and archaic forms, is very much a religion that emerges out of this special pact and a sense of obligation to the stranger-guest; according to the Gospel of James, it is a religion of strangers, orphans, and widows, all of whom lay claim to the right of *aidōs* in the name of a divine master, or host. In turn, Benveniste defines this form of absolute dependency that determines the Christian understanding of finitude as the obligation that defines a mortal creature who is literally "bound to the site" by his creator-God—that is, who becomes a "being towards death."[16] In other words, it is only according to a Christian sense of *religio* that death assumes the obligatory form of finitude, of the *ens creatum*. Consequently, the Christian owes God his or her very life to the Host; in fact, he is even a "slave to Christ," according to Paul, marking a state of absolute dependency and obligation that surpasses all worldly obligations. As a result, the very content of the term **religio** *undergoes a distinct and outward transformation, no longer designating a subjective form of inhibition or prohibition (that of "having scruples") but instead an objective oath and institutional form of "having obligations" that is reserved for a heavenly Host, or in the name of those who are bound to the same site.* Moreover, after the gradual secularization of this notion of *aidōs* (respect, reverence), the more the human being becomes "free" to exist in his or her own circle of community, one claimed by right of citizenship or birth, the more that a state of absolute dependency is especially reserved or restricted only to the religious sphere of existence. In between these two spheres, however, the obligation of hospitality can become mitigated by other interests that juridically determine it—all the way to being vanquished completely from the sphere of the political under certain circumstances and with regard to certain strangers who do not belong to the closed circle of the polis.

To conclude these reflections concerning the evolution of the social and religious institutions pertaining to the relation between the host and the stranger-guest, let us return to the earlier assertion that there is no universal species of stranger; thus, every stranger is a "particular stranger" (i.e., determined by statute or positive law). With this observation Benveniste is raising the possibility that the original guest–host relationship (the archaic or Homeric institution of hospitality) can indeed undergo transformation of its content and, as a social institution, may even cease to exist historically through the gradual rewriting of the positive statutes and laws of a given society concerning its own "particular strangers." Therefore, if every stranger is "a particular stranger," then every appearance of the stranger is completely dependent on the positive statute or law that determines his or her "recognition." The restricted and special obligations accorded to the behavioral comportment of obligatory hospitality are only the progressive and legal comportments of the same obligation, which has no natural basis, only a legal and juridical one. Here we can only briefly recall that the process of estrangement (or "depropriation") that led to the genocide of European Jews under National Socialism gradually evolved from the juridical revision of positive laws that distinguished, primarily through marriage and racial membership, between those strangers who "come from the outside" and those who belong to the closed group and are thus "copartners in the political rights" of the closed group. In other words, the language and personae that originally belonged to the archaic institution of hospitality gradually disappear from the earth and are replaced by the modern political and juridical codes of responsibility enforced only by positive laws and today, especially in the area of international law, are where the "concrete encounters" between the stranger-guest and the stranger–host relationship are primarily located. However, as has been shown, first spoken as a natural language by the members of the family and then metaphorically transposed into the spheres of religion and civil society, the language of friendship has suffered from being both poetically overdetermined within each separate sphere throughout its migration into other linguistic families (as Benveniste suggests, in the manner of a dream-work) and as having acquired a new meaning that is shorn of all sentimentality and exists only in legal–juridical language to address the situation of those "particular strangers" who belong to the modern polis. Of course, this has resulted in a number of new "concrete situations" in which there may be a particular stranger invented by these new significations but no host, no obligation, and no possibility of *aidōs* (regard, pity, mercy, sympathy in misfortune, etc.). It is this last concrete situation that also happens to address the particular stranger who is the deportee, as I discuss in the next chapter.

five

Deportee (Fr. *le déporté*)

Blessed are the poor . . .

   —Matthew 5:3

Let us now leave this bucolic Greek desert and its rustic genealogy in order to return to a more modern "concrete situation," recalling Schmitt's term, that determines the fate of those who are not recognized to share the same political rights. In its extreme form, this evokes the concrete situation of war as well as the appearance of "a particular stranger" who exists outside the closed circle of the polis, a subject who can no longer claim to share the same political rights of the natural community: the deportee.

Throughout this study, I have been evoking the possibility of a "postwar" concept of friendship, which I have also argued is still awaiting a political philosophy yet capable of thinking it.[1] To portray this concrete situation, I return to the figure of Robert Antelme, the member of the French Resistance and a survivor of Buchenwald and Dachau, who was the subject of the earlier correspondence between Deleuze and Mascolo. Antelme's earlier letters to Mascolo, written in 1945 during his period of convalescence, are the subject of Mascolo's later book written a few years after Antelme's death in 1984 and represent a continuing effort on the part of his friends to monumentalize his portrait as an act of resistance against the incredible efforts to forget the war, the existence of the camps, and the enduring (but fading) presence of those who survived this experience. Also, in Maurice Blanchot's *The Infinite Conversation,* which collects his writings between the period of 1953 to 1965, and which Deleuze himself calls a conversation between "exhausted friends," there is a meditation on Antelme's figure under the subtitle "Humankind," where we first find the statement (later on also employed by Agamben) that "man is the indestructible that can be destroyed." As Blanchot writes: "That man can be destroyed is certainly not reassuring: but because of and despite of this, and in this very movement, man should remain indestructible—this fact is truly overwhelming."[2] In the following, however, it is not the paradoxical significance of this statement that is the object of my reflections but rather the conscious certainty that Antelme expresses concerning the unity of the human species and not its destruction under the National Socialist program of extermination. In other words, it is this character of certainty alone that qualifies Antelme to become a central figure in the later writings of Blanchot and Mascolo, and perhaps this is what Deleuze had in mind when he calls Antelme a new conceptual persona of the friend, "where personal history and singular thinking combine."[3]

In the very few statements written after the publication of *The Human Species* (1947), Antelme only repeats his conviction, on the basis of his "personal experience as a deportee and a survivor," that in "a truly free society in which each man exists *as a man,* [he] exists as an end in himself."[4] In taking up this statement, we might classify the character of certainty of this knowledge as belonging to a class of concepts that Kant called a priori synthetic, except in this instance, such knowledge hails from an experience that cannot be generalized, since it could only be shared among those who survived the experience itself, the so-called survivors. In his own writings on Antelme, Blanchot constantly underlines this fact: first, the impossibility of sharing this experience through speech; second, the impossibility of thinking the unity of the concept of man *with* this experience; and third, the impossibility of the experience itself. And yet, Antelme had an unshakeable conviction that this unity has come about historically ("at the end of history") and thus already belongs to the past of our species rather than to some unknown future as it is often represented by philosophy or politics. While most post-war philosophies have busied themselves with thinking the final negation of this unity in the concept of man—that is, that the Nazis, and the SS in particular, were different, no longer quite human, but *subhuman,* and thus it was on the basis of their definition of the human life as a species-being, fundamentally determined as a racial being, that they could separate themselves from other races in order to judge them as worthy of extinction—Antelme witnessed the unity of the human species, even at its most extreme limit, since, as he claims, the SS were members of the same species (i.e., they were human like us). Consequently, in their own program to "negate the unity of the species within their own race," according to Antelme, they only managed to exhaust a division that has run its course throughout the history of scientific and racist ideologies, actually bringing about the reverse of this history as a living expression of "the unity of Man."[5]

Nevertheless, this unity cannot be represented by modern scientific disciplines of biology or anthropology, which themselves are only ideologies founded on the primacy of division and on a fundamental myth: that division fundamentally constitutes the species, and that the common (or "universal") essence can only be obtained by complete knowledge of this difference and diversity. According to this view that nature is the location of "lack" in the species, incapable of unifying the genus-being of the human species with the subjective spirit of humanity, the specific labor of the negative enters into history, defining history itself as a plane where the separation of the species and their potential unification has been played out successively over many centuries. Consequently, the idea of the common is not an idea of nature but rather the emergence of a strictly historical idea that functions to supplement nature, making up for, and thus complementing, an original deficiency. In Hegel, the unification of the species into an Absolute Subject is only achieved via the negative route introduced into the original deficiency of the natural determination of the species as a "common entity." It is something that must be produced by activity, by an active transformation of humanity as a species-being, and this activity defines both a process that is historical and the object of both political and economic systems and their associated technological "enframing" of biopolitical life.

It is also on the basis of the same primordial division, moreover, that we find that there remains implicit a nineteenth-century biologism (i.e., "Social Darwinism") even in Marx's notion of humanity as a genus that is divided against itself in the beginning, at war with its own identity as a common species-being. This is an original defect that emerges in "need" organized instinctually into forms of interest that clash with one another and become the basis of all social conflict. Consequently, the concept of the common is lacking at the level of the biological determination of the species, and it is from this lack that the multiple determinations of class division emerge historically that define the divisions of "the common property of man" until this is finally organized by neoliberal ideology into the various and diverse forms of contemporary biopolitical life. Therefore, even before Sigmund Freud, it was Marx who first declared that "biology is not destiny," to which he added that Communism was the active sprit of destiny that was the only subject capable of repairing the original lack in nature—that is, the dispersion of the "common property" of the species into multiple and unequal divisions that, in turn, distort the true forms of social need and community. Finally, if we assume, according to the thesis of Agamben, that the original social division finds its ultimate expression in the camp—that is, in the absolute division between *bios* and *zoē* in the production of "bare life"—then all remaining divisions in current society (between classes or even between races) must be understood, according to the precise term of Louis Althusser, as "survivals" (*survivants)* of this final and absolute division of the common property of man. Just as the term functioned to designate, in classical Marxist thought, the continued existence of previous social divisions that belonged to earlier stages of production, it now functions analogously to designate that all current divisions (antagonisms and exclusions) exist as so many earlier stages to the determination of this division in its final instance by technological and scientific racism that was realized by the National Socialist State. Of course, racism must be extended here from its earlier historical representations of the history of anti-Semitism that finds its culminating point in Nazi ideology, to include the new definitions addressed by Foucault's concept of biopower as a division between the forces of life, labor, and consumption that do not necessarily correspond to "subjects" (individuals, members of classes, and races) but address entire populations, or "the vast flows of humanity" (migrant labor, refugees, deportees, the poor, etc.).

In a remarkable essay published just one year after *The Human Species*, "Poor Man—Proletarian—Deportee," Antelme returns to account for the history of this species division (into classes, races, and peoples) in order to clarify its incarnation from the Christian era and leading to its culmination under National Socialism. Today, he argues in 1949, the fundamental division that runs underneath all subsequent historical incarnations is simply the universal division between rich and poor. As he writes, "This couple has become progressively anonymous in history, but the two partners remained closely linked for a long time." Accordingly, the rich man is the master who lives off the exploitation of the poor, which is the form of his worldly salvation, and in compensation works off his "evil" through the creation of charity—gifts offered to the poor in exchange for his "acts of evil," which redeems the rich man by clothing the poor in order to hide his own nakedness and social misery. As a corollary, "The poor man is destined for blessedness. . . . In the end, he becomes convinced that he will find his chance for this blessedness only in his condition as victim, as a person who is exploited, in his predetermined, sacred place within the linked couple of rich/poor."[6] In the previous Christian world, he writes:

> *The poor man was a truth himself.* He was the possibility of redemption made real. His relationship to the rich man placed him in the surest relationship to God. But this relationship was fixed, was in some sense an obligation. Salvation and *real damnation* were linked. He surpassed the rich man before God, but he relied on him, they were linked. No *truth* existed that *separated* the poor man from the rich man in this world; he did not envelop the rich man in this world but existed instead within his universe.[7]

In this last statement we might see a pronouncement of the failure of modern political dialectics to resolve the contradiction between rich and poor and to make of this opposition between rich and poor a common identity. This sets the stage for the emergence of the modern democratic subject who, according to Antelme, is both rooted in the poor by being destitute and exploited but also endowed with an active consciousness and the ability to work off his own exploitation, even by becoming the rich man to himself, which nevertheless remains a form of depropriation and negation, since the classes of poor and destitute only multiply under new forms of exploitation invented by capitalism. Thus, the concept of the poor now becomes empty and thoroughly secularized. Moreover:

> The rich/poor couple breaks apart. A truth now separates them, and it is the proletarian—who certainly didn't invent it—who wants to realize it. From a poor man who is a totally destitute being [i.e., one whose value only exists in God], he wants to erect a totally free man who is recognized as such by everyone. And he wants to universalize this value."[8]

This universal and universalizing value, as Antelme defines it later on, is humanity *as such*. Here we see the emergence of the political project of emancipation of universal democracy—in which all men would be recognized as free by everyone else—correspond to the emergent consciousness of the bourgeoisie in Marx's own analysis, as the proto-proletarian consciousness of a man liberated from the material conditions of his servitude and exploitation by an earlier class of masters, a man who works off his servitude and his destitution, who, more importantly, "clothes himself" (also symbolically meaning one who humanizes himself through his own activity and work) and who thus no longer depends on the rich man nor upon God for his own image and value as a human being. However, because the emergence of bourgeois consciousness is still rooted in the kingdom of the poor, from which he takes his morality and his "justice" in opposition to a class of former masters, he runs the risk of always falling again to the level of the poor "should his consciousness weaken or grow dim."[9] In other words, the democratic project of an emancipated humanity can exist only in the present moment within the active project of universalizing the value of man through his own activity, and this active soteriological history is now referred to the field of politics and no longer to religion and, ultimately, to the creation of the state as the concrete expression of this principle of ultimate recognition, as we also discovered in Schmitt. The modern liberal democratic state is no longer a "kingdom of ends" but rather a "kingdom of rights" and a purveyor of recognition. Thus, the form of universal recognition that is performed by the state is thoroughly temporalized and thus refers only to the present time, having neither history nor eternity. That is, the democratic state exists in such a manner that it demands recognition from everyone in every present moment; moreover, the nature of this social demand is enforced: should this consciousness of recognition weaken or falter, it would then be seen as a threat to the security of the identity on which the community is founded. As for the liberal democratic project, as well as for the socialist, should this historical dialectic ever stop, even for one moment, and admit its failure to realize this value "for all human beings and all divisions" (including animals who belong to its kingdom), then the subject could quickly find himself again in the situation of the poor, stripped of an active consciousness, passively accepting his natural condition of a being who is located at a certain level of poverty by a force that resembles fate or predetermination in their original Greek senses.

It is at this point, however, in what appears as a third dialectical reversal surrounding the conceptual personage of the deportee, that Antelme addresses the historical incarnation of this division in its final instance between the SS-master and the deportee-enemy. In contradiction to the previous incarnation of the rich–poor couple, the SS embodies the position of the rich man who no longer needs the poor man as a path for his own salvation *in this world*; as Antelme observes, "The SS wanted to kill all their *poor men*."[10] Consequently, there was no longer any identification with the poor man, since in the earlier Christian phase the rich were obliged to recognize the value of the poor man in God and thus were equally obliged to clothe their naked bodies and feed them in order to compensate for their own evil; this was the exact price of their salvation *in this world.* Before the SS, however, the poor man was no longer a man—and was certainly not a sacred man—but was simply determined as an enemy of the rich, "and the more oppressed he was the less chance he had of being a man."[11] Here, according to Antelme's dialectical thesis, for the first time the link that bound the anonymous couple, rich man/poor man, was broken and could no longer be repaired by any shared morality; *rich and poor appeared as two entirely different species-beings who, from that point onward, had no common relationship except that of being mortal enemies.* "In light of this extreme situation in the link between rich and poor," Antelme writes, "we understand how impossible it is to fill in the concept of the 'poor man' from any point of view that is not strictly phenomenological."

> From the moment, in fact, when the couple rich/poor, exploiter/ exploited, protector/protected—whatever you like—is broken apart by the awakening of consciousness in the exploited, the poor man has ceased to exist as such, except as the enemy of all poor men. When the poor man has become a proletarian, the rich man has become the SS. And when the rich man has become the SS, the poor man, who remained a *poor man, cannot* remain in the same situation of poor man; he has become an enemy of the proletariat, or else he has immediately agreed to his own death.[12]

It is at this point in history we witness the awakening of the consciousness of the deportee, who still remains an enemy of the rich but from a point of view that no longer corresponds to the former position of the poor man or the destitute and exploited position of the proletarian consciousness. The concrete situation of the deportee is presented in the form of a double bind (either you remain a poor man and become an enemy to yourself or you must agree to your own death), and it is from this double bind that a new consciousness is produced. This emergent, new consciousness is a product of the refusal of the order of the SS; consequently, the deportee was no longer a poor man, who found his value in God, nor even the bourgeoisie or the avatar of the working-class proletariat who sought to work off this division through the humanization of the universe (and thus project the complete redemption of man in the future of a political order) but instead found the certainty of his consciousness as a man in the active refusal of a complete negation of his own value as a member of the same species.

> There did not exist a single believing deportee who, on again hearing Christ's message—"Blessed are the poor"—did not think, did not immediately cry out, the complete, the true meaning of that message: that the SS order, the order of the rich, represented the negation of man, and had to be combated.[13]

Therefore, "merely to wish to live—but standing side by side with the deportees—was enough to make a proletarian, a man who actively refused the SS project to make him die, a proletarian on the same level as the universal, because the freedom of all men was tied to his victory, to his survival."[14] It is this character of certainty in the recognition of consciousness that emerged in the camp, in the subject of the deportee and the survivor. It is only in this last statement that we can begin to understand Antelme's radical thesis that the SS incarnated the final instance (and the exhaustion) of all the previous species divisions and, as a result, unconsciously restored to the idea of the human the concrete certainty of its unity as a species-being. This might even take the form of a Christological determination of a new human being; although, it is a figure that replaces the previous Christian form.

Again, following this quasi-Hegelian logic, we must understand this character of certainty and this consciousness historically as the embodiment of the spirit (or mind) that cannot be reversed and represents a culmination of the recognition of freedom out of a concrete expression of consciousness itself, no longer in the form of a dependence on the master or by his own activity of labor or work. It is only at this extreme point that a subject emerges as a universal value that must now be recognized by everyone. The true historical consciousness of the survivor, from this point onward, would only be identified with this great refusal of a project that would make someone die but also would be the sharpened consciousness of an enemy: an enemy of the rich. It is for this reason that there can no longer be any common or shared morality between the rich and the poor, no universal religion, no system of charity that could cover over or save the rich man from his own evil in this world. Once again, we find a claim that was later taken up as a major thesis by Agamben, who did not always credit Antelme as the original source: "We believe that we have revealed, or recognized, that there is no inherent difference between the 'normal' system of man's exploitation and that of the camps. The camps are simply a sharpened image of the more-or-less hidden hell in which most people still live"; therefore, "we cannot accept any morality or any value if it cannot be made concretely universal."[15]

Concerning Antelme's final thesis, however, we cannot help but note that the final stage of this dialectic does not resolve itself into a synthesis. In fact, it does quite the opposite: it completes the original division between rich and poor and carries out their opposition, which becomes an absolute opposition. It splits the two terms into an irreparable antagonism. In other words, this division is no longer cast in the form of a contradiction that could be concealed or otherwise "redeemed" by any moral or political system. There is no salvation in this world, or the next, for the rich man who becomes completely identified with the SS. From here onward, outside the earlier division, the "rich man" no longer establishes a genus either determined by the classic division of labor or by the species-being of racism that resolves this earlier contradiction. Instead, the rich man determines a new form of biopolitical life that is now absolutely opposed to the existence of the poor. As for the sacred poor, according to Antelme's own thesis, either he has completely disappeared, or is faced with an impossible decision, for the poor man who chooses to remain a poor man thereby becomes an enemy to himself. Concretely, as the result of either decision, the sacred position of the poor man in the universe disappears entirely, since if he chooses to remain a member of the sacred poor, he must willingly agree to his own extermination as part of this divine order. And yet, Antelme already refutes this last possibility, since no deportee would have ever accepted their fate under order of the SS as God's commandment. In the above passage, I am simply underscoring the historical meaning of Antelme's earlier claim that the poor man disappears entirely. It is not just that, by definition, the poor disappeared because they were exterminated in the camps but also that the position of the poor vis-à-vis "the rich SS" was no longer possible or even thinkable. Underlining this disappearance is also the fact that the idea of the poor as the "sacred being" who is sanctified and blessed by God for his sacrifice and his poverty disappears as well. Thus the poor man is placed in a deadly paradox: either to become an enemy to himself by consciously agreeing to his own death, which is impossible even to think; or, instead, to choose "bare life," in which case the poor man has no real choice except to condemn himself to death (i.e., to become the SS to himself).

Here again, what Antelme is calling our attention to is the complete exhaustion of a certain "morality" that has been built up around the figure of the poor for centuries, first by Judaism and then by Christianity, which divinizes the sacred being of the poor as a form of blessedness, "Blessed are the poor" (Matthew 5:3). In part, this morality has been responsible for sanctifying the victims of poverty and exploitation with a false consciousness of innocence for the evil that is inflicted on them by the rich. In other words, we must understand that the SS, who embody the extreme or "sharpened" position of all the masters who have preceded them, have also pushed the dialectic to a breaking point, since by refusing any recognition of commonality with the poor, which they must exterminate to the last man, they have also become the SS to the man in themselves. In other words, no morality can emerge to *do justice* to their evil unless it is the rationalization of total war against all the poor and the proletariat. This is their consciousness and their certainty. Ironically, however, they embody the extreme weakness and inherent flaw that was already present in the consciousness of the bourgeoisie, since the certainty of this consciousness can only exist as long as their power of extermination and division of the species is actualized in the camps, and thus this consciousness would disappear from the earth entirely the moment when the extermination is halted, as was certainly realized at the end of the war when Hitler ordered the extermination of the German people themselves for failing to achieve the order of the Reich. And the consciousness of the bourgeois is perverted from its objective of the universalization of the value of man to the purification of the race defined by the SS. Once this horrible labor of the negative was halted, this consciousness historically disappeared as well, along with the grotesque idea that the poor who accepted their fate of extermination remained in a state of blessedness, who were not simply killed and disposed of as bare life. In other words, the idea of the sacred poor was extinguished along with the idea of the sacred race.

Perhaps we are now in a position to understand what Antelme now claims as the victory of the survivor. If we remember, the poor disappeared by virtue of the fact that if they chose to remain poor, to claim the position of the sacred man in the camps, they must agree with their own extermination—but this is impossible and is presented in the form of contradiction or logical impossibility. As we say in the earlier passage, there was no deportee who willingly agreed to his own death. At the same time, the masters embodied a form of consciousness whose certainty remained only as long as the active technopolitical–scientific project of extermination was carried out and thus also disappeared from the earth the moment they failed to carry out this program completely— that is, to realize the unity of their race through the complete extermination of all their poor. It is only the survivor who remains by refusing equally the role of sacred victim *(homo sacer)* as well as the willing accomplice to the negation of man within himself (the SS), thus surviving the double negation of both rich and poor. If this sounds like a synthesis, it is only through the negation of the previous oppositions that it is achieved. As one consequence, however, for the survivor, "bare life" or "merely living" can no longer be called sacred. *If only from the perspective and the concrete experience of the survivor,* life (or concretely, what life that remains to be lived) can no longer be sanctified by God, and there is no suffering that can any longer be tolerated or justified as sacred. There is no morality that can justify the extreme situation of the camp, which now stands as the concrete symbol (or paradigm) for all exclusion; therefore, from this point onward, all suffering, all oppression, as well as all poverty, can only be identified with the conscious certainty of an active refusal to any longer negate the man within himself— that is to say, from a living spirit of "combat."

In this final incarnation of the dialectic, we might recognize the situation that continues today around the growing demographic of another spirit of refusal globally and by a new class of poor who have emerged to assume the position once occupied by the sacred poor. This spirit of refusal first emerged in the accusation, addressed to the rich, that these acts of charity were only made in compensation for their misery. In place of the former poor, according to Antelme's final observation, the rich are now faced by those who are united by their refusal of such charity and whose "recognition" only defiles the peaceful image of humanity created by the rich to hide their own normal system of exploitation, which has only served to consign the largest portion of this humanity to the real hell in which most people still live today.

Antelme writes: "We believe we have revealed, or recognized, that there is no inherent difference between the 'normal' system of exploitation and that of the camps. That the camps are simply a sharpened image of the more or less hidden hell in which most people still live."[16] As a result, and already foreshadowing our current situation, he concludes:

> Faced with this poor man who arrived at consciousness, the rich man goes crazy. The object of charity gives way; humanity, for him, is transformed. The proletarian haunts the world, and the world is defiled: yellow, black, Jews, communists, Christians, those never before *seen,* pour forth—men who say no, *subhumans.*[17]

Therefore, if the rich today have been driven insane and are haunted by the proletarian consciousness and its refusal to accept the situation that has been determined for them under the system of wealth, it is possibly because the classes of subhumans are seemingly infinite and emerge from too many places in the world today. It is no longer the case where the poor man cannot encompass the rich man's world but resides in his universe *but rather it is the insane rich man who has come to realize that he resides in the universe that is being created by these very same subhuman classes and that his own position of security in this new order is far from certain.* Perhaps, like the historical failure of the bourgeoisie, he will come to occupy a position of weakened consciousness and find himself once again in the position of the poor, deprived of the very world he has made by his own hands—that is, unless the rich hang onto their narrowing position by waging a perpetual war against all the poorest populations in the world.

In response to this worsening situation, it is not surprising to see today the incredible conversion to Christianity especially among the very rich populations in the First World but precisely as a kind of nostalgic return to reestablishing a relationship of a pastoral form of sovereignty and charity toward the disaffected and proletarianized poor and subhuman classes that they have created in the first place. And yet, this will not work, for the reasons already recounted above following Antelme's thesis. Any attempt to address the growing demographic of the global poor—at least, to administer their populations through a concerted "letting die"—will only provide the conditions for the awakening of consciousness similar to the deportee, for the creation of a new enemy. Moreover, as shown by recent global events, this is because the spirit of refusal on the part of a new *poor man* no longer assumes the form of politics but rather the return of an absolute and Manichean order of "good and evil." In fact, according to Antelme's early thesis, this is the ultimate destination of the original division of rich and poor; however, it exceeds any political and economic rationalism and marks the absolute limit where both political and economic powers today have reached a threshold of postmodernity that cannot be addressed by a secularized ideal of the universal but rather only ameliorated in the interest of globalized security and the protection of free markets, which are strictly defined in juridical and economic terms and no longer in terms of a single or unified image of humanity or according to the democratic ideal of a universal friendship.

At this point I return to the idea of friendship that, at least for Mascolo and Blanchot, is instituted around the figure of Antelme. In the correspondence that occurs later between Antelme and Mascolo, the idea of friendship is no longer defined in positive terms. In a letter written in 1950, Antelme writes:

> I don't think of friendship as something positive, as a value I mean; but instead I think of it far more as a state, an identification, a multiplication of death, a multiplication of questioning, as miraculously the most neutral of places from which to grasp and to feel the constant of the unknown . . . the proximity to death. It is the questioning that I think first of all, or the cry of the impossible.[18]

Here, in other words, we might see the return of a more archaic notion of friendship that we addressed in the previous section, which is particularly reserved for those who are deprived of all political rights, for those subhuman classes who emerge around the impossible cry of *aidōs* (dignity, respect) but for whom there is no longer any corresponding host—that is, no modern institution of hospitality. Thus, Blanchot and Mascolo both speak of an exigency that only the deportee and survivor can testify to from the extremity of an experience that is impossible to communicate, and thus it is only the survivor who is given any authority over this speech, "the unique authority of this speech coming directly from this exigency."[19] For Mascolo, Antelme's exigency had but one revelation: "The organization of society into classes, such as we experience it in our daily lives, was already an image of the division of this same society into species, such as it existed in the society created in the camps."[20] Therefore, "scientific racism," which marks the culmination of both the technological rationalism and philosophical nationalism of the post-Enlightenment societies of which German society was the most extreme expression, is only the embodiment of class division in its

last or "final instance." As Antelme writes: "It's an SS fantasy to believe
that we have an historical mission to change species, and as this mutation is slowly occurring, they kill. No, this extraordinary sickness is
nothing other than a culminating moment in man's history."[21] Elsewhere, Mascolo says that this is the very basis of *our communism* from
that point onward, in the sense that "the intuition of the unity of the
species naturally leads to the historical necessity of the communist idea,
which is no longer for that reason solely political."[22] Again, I underline
that this intuition is neither a political nor religious idea, nor is it a
theory of political economy of the division of the species that is scientific in nature, since all the disciplines themselves belong to the history
of this division and were partly responsible for its final transformation
into racism. In other words, as Mascolo argues, the modern disciplines
have only rendered archaic myths of "the inequality of the races" more
presentable in the form of new scientific and anthropological *epistemes*
and thus in a much more dangerous fashion (more possible and thinkable) that we scarcely any longer need to recover these earlier myths
in order to find nationalism far more preferable as, for example, the
response to terror has recently shown. However, in the face of terror we
cannot find peace in the reduction of social order to a single and total-
izing model, whether this assumes a hegemonic super-state *(Pax Ameri-
cana)* or the economic hegemony of the current neoliberal order, which
I have argued earlier can only be regarded as a "generalized Machiavellianism." In fact, such are the alternatives still offered today regardless
of whether the preference is neoliberal or democratic: either newly
emergent expressions of nationalism and ethnocentrism or the justification of a permanent hegemonic struggle between populations *without even the idea of perpetual peace as a horizon*—and thus the endless
production of new classes and new divisions to the coming war. (Again,
I simply underscore the fact that today what we are witnessing is a spirit
of refusal and a new form of combat whose horizon cannot be defined
in political terms, which poses the greatest threat to any political constitution of humanity or any pretension of the idea of universal democracy.) Concerning the future of this new hegemonic struggle, it appears

that the state of permanent warfare has been accepted by neoliberal society and leftist critics alike, since the former cannot affirm the idea of communism as an absolute future, and the latter cannot admit to a democratic alternative due to the failures of late-capitalist democracies, and thus both have fatally resigned themselves to accepting the position that all politics are partial and thus condemned to repeat an endless cycle of appropriation/depropriation. *This either/or is, ultimately, the impasse and the final exhaustion of the concept of the political itself:* neither nationalism, which is unthinkable by virtue of its absolute culminating point in Nazism, nor any solution to the possible end of a more generalized hegemonic struggle for power, which culminates in a political form that is governed according to the accepted premise that the cycle of violence and depropriation, is inevitable (if not necessary). At best, all we can hope is to find a better way to manage and administer the original species division as the only measure of peace that can be imagined for the future of humanity, which Deleuze and Guattari have argued might actually bring about a state of peace "more terrifying than fascist death."[23]

We have now come to the end of this dialectic. The terms have split apart and become irreparable. The two halves of the broken ring of friendship have been destroyed by perpetual war. Concerning the destination of *phílos,* just as the original signification of the Homeric Greek terms became, already by the time of Euripides's Medea in the fifth century BCE, the ceremonial and hollow terms to be employed strategically for temporary alliance and economic advantage, today the politics of friendship have become totally corrupted by capital and there appears to be no future political form that seems capable of establishing a truce between two immortal enemies: the global rich and the global poor. Again, the rich man can no longer pretend "to clothe and feed" the poor in a total act of friendship and modesty, particularly after dismantling the welfare state, abandoning his "own poor"; nor can he conceal from himself the evil of the world of poverty his wealth has created, which returns to visit terror on him from the outside and threaten his security. It may very well be the case that for some the image of a "weakened sense" of religion (in opposition to an archaic or sovereign form of

Islamic fundamentalism) is a new source of hope for renewing a more pastoral form of liberal democratic ideals of universal fraternity and/or friendship, but it is also evident that the new universe created by the poor and subaltern classes globally may have no place reserved for the rich. Instead, we might recall as a warning the statement of Achilles to Hector:

> Do not propose an agreement. There are no pledges *(hórkia pistá)* between lions and men. The hearts of wolves and sheep do not beat in unison, but constantly do they devise evil for each other; even so is it not possible for you and me to be in *philótēs,* and there will be no *hórkia* between us: *emè kaì sè philḗmenai oudé ti nôin hórkia éssontai* (until the moment when one or the other is killed).[24]

In response to this pledge, as Antelme promises, the rich man (representing the advanced nations of the world) can only go insane and cling to his increasingly narrowing demographic, which is diminishing more and more each day, and thus it seems that he has also become a survivor in the universe he has created. Thus, at the point of closure of this complex genealogy, we come to three figures that stem from the modern experiences of amnesia and aphasia that have placed friendship in "distress": first, we have the various contemporary strangers and new classes of subhumans who appear today in the very center of the polis as those *who have been deprived of all their political rights*; second, we have all those survivors who have passed through an experience of war and perhaps represent the "concrete situation" of the refugee populations today who live "in a more-or-less hidden hell" (i.e., a precarious existence deprived of both political rights and nationhood, at the mercy of their national hosts); and finally, we have the dominating figure of the global poor who can no longer be called "blessed," or clothed by the charity of the richest nations. It is this last figure, moreover, and the increasing demographic it represents, who is becoming the wellspring of terrorism and thus regarded with renewed fear and suspicion. And for that reason the global poor will continue to be condemned to live outside the broken circle of friendship, in the wastelands that lie beyond the hedges: in the encampments and "security zones" of the richest populations in history (who are nevertheless decreasing in their own demographic proportion, necessarily as a result).[25] In other words, today there is no possibility for any political philosophy, much less any new "concept of the political," that does not address at its beginning these three figures as the new conceptual personae who will determine the future compass and the extreme limit of *our common species*.

six

A Revolutionary People
(Fr. *la machine de guerre*)

A relapse into barbarism is always an option.

—Theodor Adorno, *Toward a New Manifesto*

Finally, let us return now to the war *(pólemos)*. As we recall from our earlier discussion of "the enemy" *(der Feind)*, Plato never admits its comparison with the forms of struggle and competition that could occur between citizens—that is, with the indigenous forms of conflict *(stásis)* belonging to the polis; therefore, he even sought to banish the legality of civil war from the Republic and compared it to "self-laceration," the willful destruction of one's own organs, or body proper.[1] It is around this metaphor of the body that we discover a second image of the exteriority of violence in opposition to the internal conflicts that maintain the social cohesion of the group. By contrast, the nature of violence defined by the term *pólemos* is characterized by its "exteriority" with regard to the body proper (i.e., the internal precincts of the city-state), which also entails a violence that cannot be internalized as a conservative function of state power. In other words, war represents a violence that is always directed outward, away from the body proper, specifically aimed at the destruction of the organs of a foreign body (or host). As already discussed, in order to poetically identify the location of this foreign body Plato often employs the term "barbarian" *(barbaros)* and, on other occasions, "the natural enemy" (i.e., the Persian).

With regard to the two species of violence, as Deleuze and Guattari argue, historically the state form has employed only two choices in order to distinguish between them: first, it fashions a special part of its own apparatus that is specifically invented to apply a certain expression of violence that is directed against its own citizens (i.e., its police forces, its prisons, its judges, its teachers and bureaucrats; basically, all those functionaries who are made responsible for both maintaining and reproducing the various kinds of state violence); second, it must acquire an army *(une armée)*.[2] Accordingly, the existence of the war machine is not intrinsic to the form of state power itself, since the function of state power is to conserve and to protect, even to replenish, the organs of state power; whereas the nature of the violence deployed by the war machine is not conservative but essentially destructive, since its sole objective is to destroy the enemy by laying waste to his organs, thus preventing him to either conserve or reproduce his own body proper.

For example, concerning the first species, even the violence inflicted by the police, the courts, or even prisons is made to conserve a form of state power. Crime is treated by a form of violence that seeks to either repress or to correct its inherent contradiction to the principles of law and order. The activity of the criminal represents the expression of conflict that must be dialectically remedied in order to restore the principle of identity, and it is not by chance that the form of violence or repression is made to be equivalent to that initial expression: the robber is stripped of all his possessions and imprisoned; the murderer is executed. Although crime certainly represents a form of exteriority, defined as a concrete instance of contradiction that appears against the abstract law, through the organs of state power (its police, courts, prisons, and executioners) the concrete and external existence of conflict is canceled out and the contradiction is "peacefully" resolved in the identification of the criminal with the crime. In this manner, productive violence restores unity to the normally abstract principle of law by giving it a concrete instance of identity in which it can bathe itself anew, by revitalizing its own organs and restoring their function to the choral unity of the body proper. "Order is beautiful" *(kalos)* and thus becomes the primary virtue of the city, the first and most primitive of all the state forms.

It is for this reason, turning now to the second species of violence, that Deleuze and Guattari come to the conclusion that "provisionally speaking, the war machine is first invented by the nomads," since as they claim, the state itself certainly does not invent war (being itself only "an empty form of appropriation"), and so it appears that the violence of *pólemos* is not only exterior with regard to state power but also exists much earlier and thus appears more primitive as well. "In every respect," Deleuze and Guattari write, "the war machine is of another species, another nature, another origin than the State apparatus."[3] Moreover, we find that there is always something essentially lawless, random, undisciplined, and, most importantly, nondialectical about war and especially those lonely and exceptional figures who have emerged through the fog of wars and who can even appear as exterior to the form of power favored by the state. Moreover, it is precisely this lawless and solitary conceptual persona of a revolutionary people that also becomes a key feature of Deleuze and Guattari's concept of the war machine *(la machine de guerre)*.

In their "Treatise on Nomadology," Deleuze and Guattari provide a detailed account of the long history of the appropriation of the war machine by the state form, and it is here that we find frequent references to the solitary, exceptional, and even suicidal characters like Homer's Achilles or Heinrich von Kleist's Michael Kolhaas and Penthesilea. Why? To be exceptional or "alone" means in some way to be found outside the circle of society (and often against it) but not in any way that could be compared to the criminal who merely represents the law's own internal contradiction (which can be peacefully resolved). By contrast, the warrior who kills himself in one suicidal act, destroying his own organs, represents a kind of violence that cannot ultimately be internalized by the state form, despite its efforts to recoup this suicidal character of violence in the myths of martyrdom or patriotic sacrifice. Nevertheless, something always remains exterior and excessive in these acts or in the exceptional individuals who become capable of undergoing them, even to the point of representing a form of exteriority that can assume what Deleuze elsewhere defines as a "terrible supersensible Primary Nature that knows no Law."[4] Therefore, to be "alone," or solitary, also represents another form of individuation that is not consistent with the forms that can be found within the state. This form of individuation, as Deleuze and Guattari explain, need not be numerically defined but can also be the individuality of a pack, a band, a minority, and, finally, *a revolutionary people*. In other words, like the solitary figure of the warrior, can a people also be found to exhibit the contradictory traits of lawlessness and even, occasionally, suicide? That is, a people can fashion itself into a war machine precisely in order to expel or to ward off the state form, as Deleuze and Guattari claim (following the thought of sociologist Pierre Clastres); however, they only end up alone, wandering on the outside, distributed across a vast open space that lies between states (like a steppe or desert) but gradually disappearing from the face of the earth—that is, a people who commit suicide (or are "gradually led to suicide by society") after a long struggle or ordeal.[5]

Here we find a romantic image of a people that has often been ascribed to Deleuze and Guattari's conceptual personae of the nomad and the "becoming-minor." Of course, one can find a similar version of this image in movies and historical docudramas, especially depicting aboriginal peoples who first encounter the state form, leading eventually to struggle and then a kind of gradual suicide after a "long trail of tears," as if accepting their own fate as a people and disappearing from the face of the earth. As Deleuze and Guattari write, as the result of each new extermination and genocidal act, the war machine never fails to create new quantities: "the extermination of a minority engenders a minority of that minority."[6] Nevertheless, one can see that this kind of epic representation of "a people who are missing" clearly belongs to the state form, and the gradual (i.e., historical) and, above all, voluntary suicide can be understood as representing, from its own point of view, a relatively "peaceful" solution to the problem of new quantities. On the other hand, this nostalgic and essentially romantic image of "a people who are missing" has, as its natural double, the Messianic image of "a people still to come." This latter image has a long history and is usually ascribed to religions and to the storytelling function of subjugated and colonized peoples, but it also has an abstract representation in contemporary post-Marxist philosophy. And yet, were not Deleuze and Guattari also talking about real peoples, and is there not something essentially risky and inherently contradictory in the concept of a revolutionary people today? It seems many want to ignore this contradictory and often volatile aspect in their portrait of a people who are either found to be missing or still to come. Either we have the sad and tragic image of an oppressed or colonized people or the saintly and otherworldly image of a super-proletariat. In other words, all the possibilities of real violence are subtracted as the condition of both representations; either a people are purely subjected to violence of the state form or they are composed of a completely different nature like those marvelous and enlightened peoples we often encounter in science fiction.

By contrast, what I am suggesting is that the conceptual persona of "a revolutionary people" that we find in Deleuze and Guattari's writings bears the same bipolar (or schizoid) characteristics that they also ascribe to the war machine. For example, here is the conclusion of their "Treatise on Nomadology," where this bipolar tendency is stated with unmistakable clarity:

> The difference between the two poles is great, even, and especially, from the point of view of death: the line of flight that creates, or turns into a line of destruction; the plane of consistency that constitutes itself, even piece by piece, or turns into a plan(e) of organization and domination. We are constantly reminded that there is communication between these two lines of planes, that each takes nourishment from the other, borrows from the other: the worst of world war machines reconstitutes a smooth space to surround and enclose the earth. But the earth asserts its own powers of deterritorialization, its lines of flight, and its smooth spaces that live and blaze a way for a new earth. The question is not one of quantities but of the incommensurable character of qualities that

confront one another in the two kinds of war machine, according to the two poles.[7]

I return to comment on the above passage below, but for now I want to recall my earlier question: Does this mean, then, that the people share the same species, nature, and origin as the war machine?

In responding to this question, I might first propose this equivalence in the following manner: just as the state has no war machine of its own, since it is of "another species, another nature, another origin than the state apparatus," we can also say that the state has no people of its own—that is, being itself an "empty form of appropriation."[8] We might find the above hypothesis confirmed when we realize that the state form entertains a relationship with the people that runs parallel to the predicament it faces with its own war machine, one of exteriority and occasionally extreme volatility. First of all, the people are always posited as being "outside" the state form and, in some sense, precede its arrival and accompany the stages of its development all the way to the future in which the people are yet to actually arrive. Second, just as in the case of the war machine, the state does not create "a people" but rather attempts to internalize already existing peoples, even though this existence may be purely virtual and nomadically distributed across an open space or territory that precedes the arrival of the state form.

It is the specific mythology created by the state form that attempts to reverse this precedence by turning the people into an "idea" that first occurs in the mind of those subjects who are already found to be internal to the state form. (This is the myth of the Founding Fathers, for example, when they say, "We, the people . . .") At the same time, this might allow us to perceive the inherent problem of political idealism and utopian thinking: the failure of a people to truly arrive, because of the internalization of the people into the form of the state. This was equally the problem of fascism as it is of the idealism of the democratic state; consequently, it should not come as a surprise that Hitler ordered the German people to join him in an act of suicide for their failure in realizing the Reich. By contrast, in its late-democratic form, the state entertains a fundamentally ambivalent relationship with its own people, one that is often prone to become extremely volatile. There are always too many resisting elements, too many numbers; but even worse, the people are always failing to live up to the democratic ideals of the state— either lacking altogether or exhibiting the tendency to go a little insane, returning to religion and the authority of the family, or, if pushed to the extreme limit, becoming terrorists or serial killers.[9] In saying this, I realize that this last association has become extremely inconvenient today in relation to the image of the suicide bomber, the member of an anomalous terrorist cell who walks into a public square to explode his own organs precisely in an effort, it seems, to ward off a certain state form. In this context we might recall Arendt's prescient observation that it is "isolation" and not merely loneliness that becomes a breeding ground for terror, whether this form of isolation refers to the archaic figure of the sovereign, the sacred victim, or the (self-)isolation of an entire people as the result of the "logicality of ideological thinking" of racist exceptionalism or religious fundamentalism.[10] Moreover, there is no natural form of isolation, since every state of exception must be politically and ideologically contrived (also recalling the statement by Benveniste quoted earlier that every stranger is a particular and hence there is "no stranger *as such*").

At this point I turn to the brief, albeit infamous, commentary by Foucault on the Iranian Revolution that can be understood to raise a similar question concerning the people and the war machine.[11] It is in this text that Foucault first speaks to the "enigma of revolts" that are "outside history" and also within an official history that fails to grasp their real causality. As he argues, over the last two hundred years a quasi-scientific theory of "revolution" has been created "in a gigantic effort to domesticate revolts within a rational and controllable history: it gave them a legitimacy, separated their good forms from their bad, and defined the laws of their unfolding; it set their prior conditions, objectives, and defined the laws of their unfolding . . . a marvelous and formidable promise."[12] But what happens, Foucault asks, when a people actually revolt? Here we can see the same dilemma announced above under the concept of democracy: the failure of a people to actualize the ideals already ascribed to them by "history." In other words, they revolt in the wrong way, often by turning back to religion with its "promises of the afterlife, time's renewal, anticipation of the savior or the empire of the last days" (which also have their secularized versions in the various scientific theories of revolutions as well).[13] Foucault's criticism is aimed at the traditional leftist intelligentsia and its classical antipathy toward the people who do not resist power according to their prescriptions. Is it any wonder that the traditional Left shares the same fundamental antipathy toward the people as do most bureaucrats and jurists, which is why most leftist critics tend to err on the side of proposing some alternative version of the politburo? *At least an intensely ambivalent relationship, sometimes even a hatred of the people that already exist—is this not the historical legacy of the Left?* Moreover, is this not also the reason for the constant calls for the creation of "another people" that would replace the people that are always found to be missing (i.e., lacking in their own existence)? Of course, Deleuze and Guattari share in Foucault's criticism of the Left, particularly in their complete rejection of the concept of ideology, which they regard as an alibi that functions to preserve an idealistic image and essentially good nature of a people prior to the trappings of power and desire. Nevertheless, invoking the statement by Wilhelm Reich, they constantly claim that the people were not duped or tricked into endorsing fascism or racism, or in dedicating their own organs to the destructive war machine. In fact, recent events have shown that the people who are missing can be quite mad; therefore, to echo the statement made by Max Horkheimer, maybe real revolution is less than desirable.[14] It is for these reasons that in the future we must construct a more realistic and sober portrayal of the conceptual personage of "the revolutionary people" as a fundamental component of political philosophy.

Returning now to a second point of comparison between Foucault's earlier remarks and Deleuze and Guattari's observations on the war machine, in addition to defining revolt by a form of exteriority, Foucault also defines a people as "a singularity," which might also resemble

Deleuze and Guattari's exceptional or monomaniacal individuality—a "rogue," as Derrida would say, following Kant's remark in *Toward Perpetual Peace* (i.e., "let justice reign even if all the rogues should perish"). As Foucault writes, "People do revolt; that is a fact. That is how subjectivity (not that of great men, but that of anyone) is brought into history, breathing life into it."[15] Thus, "a singularity revolts," despite that we do not know what form a real revolt will take. In Deleuze and Guattari's writings, we are given several images of "exceptional individuals" who revolt, most of which are drawn from literary personae. Michael Kolhaas mounts his horse and sets off in a struggle he has already lost from the beginning. Ahab revolts against the white whale. These two species or types, in fact, may represent the two extreme poles of revolt in Deleuze and Guattari's writings—between the monumental portraits of Ahab (or Moby-Dick), Kleist's Penthesilea, and Richard III. Consequently, there is more than a little Shakespearean resonance to Deleuze's use of these various figures, in particular, to portray the "world-historical" characteristics of the people they are made to portray. Taken together, in fact, I would argue that these figures represent "a people" in various states of revolt, or of "becoming-revolutionary," including the state of war when a people assume the nature of a war machine.

For example, I have found no more truthful and realistic portrait of the American people than the one offered by Deleuze in his 1989 appendix to Herman Melville's "Bartleby, the Scrivener." Here we find two figures, each of which represents the extreme poles of becoming that define the American people: the monomaniacal figure of Ahab (or Moby-Dick, the Great White Whale of American imperialism) and the anomalous figure of Bartleby, the minor functionary who "prefers not to" perform his assigned or allotted role in the division of labor. Concerning ourselves only with the first pole, why is it that Deleuze always underlines the event of betrayal, "the breaking of a pact or bond," as if stepping over a certain abstract line, or going too far, as the most essential aspect of this figure? In choosing to pursue Moby-Dick, Ahab must break a pact and betray the whaler's law, which says that the violence unleashed in the hunting of whales must always be rationalized by its productive, economic justification; above all, it must never become an "object" in itself, apart from this rationalized, legal ground. (It is only in strict observance of this law, moreover, that God will "bless the harvest.") How, then, do we understand the violence of Ahab? Is this not an image of revolt, if not absolute war? Does Ahab's vengeance not express the kind of violence remarked by Deleuze and Guattari where the war machine takes war as its direct object and, in doing so, introduces a form of exteriority to any law that is so extreme in its own justification that it surpasses mere contradiction and introduces the figure of an "innately deprived being"—that is, a form of stupidity that surpasses mere ignorance and a spirit of real malice that is beyond good and evil? And yet, returning to the usual portrayal of the people, we must ask: Was Ahab absolutely alone? Did he not also share this primary nature with his crew who follow him to his death, who touch the burning lance and make a blood pact with the demonic Ahab? Were the seamen simply duped? Or rather, does this constitute one of the poles of any "revolutionary becoming"? It is because of the existence of this pole that the pilot of any revolution tends to steer toward war, as if it constituted the position of true north on the compass.

I turn now to a text where Deleuze paints a similar portrait of the Palestinian people by invoking the figure of Yasser Arafat, "like something straight out of Shakespeare."[16] Like Foucault's earlier statement on the Iranian Revolution, this has in some ways become a scandalous text. It is from September 1983, written in response to the 1982 massacre of Sabra and Shatila and condemned by some for its hints of anti-Semitism.[17] In his remarks, Deleuze's first observation concerns the failure to recognize the Palestinians as a people like any other; rather, they are only recognized as "the Arab populations that occupy Palestine" and "who have ended up there by chance or by accident" as justification for the plans for the "depopulation" of the territory.[18] In the context of these events and the history that preceded them, Deleuze asks: How do the Palestinians resist, being both outside of their territory and without a state? It is here that he evokes the exceptional figure of Arafat as "the grand historical character like something directly out of Shakespeare!"[19] Thus, Arafat represents this solitary figure or rogue who becomes the living persona of "a people who revolt." (Of course, it goes without saying that this was not a convenient image for some, given that Arafat was also an organizer of worldwide terrorism at this moment.) And yet, Deleuze's allusion to Shakespeare allows us to interpret the figure of Arafat alongside the figures that also appear in the appendix on Melville written around the same period in the mid-1980s. In other words, like the monomaniacal figure of Ahab, the figure of Arafat should be accurately conveyed so that it retains its bipolar and essentially ambiguous characteristics, which would be consistent with the war machine he represents.

By means of this allusion, Deleuze is not comparing Arafat to the mythological and romanticized image of the magical sovereign; Arafat is not King Arthur. Rather, his figure would more resemble that of Richard III, who emerges from the same violence, murder, and perversion that so often accompanies the production of good kings, to create a bastard lineage. As Deleuze and Guattari write, "A disturbing character like Richard III slips in, announcing from the outset his intention to reinvent a war machine and impose its line (deformed, treacherous and traitorous, claiming a 'secret close intent' totally different from the conquest of State Power)," which is to say, different from a line of state domination.[20] If this was the Shakespearean figure Deleuze had in mind in reference to Arafat at precisely this "world-historical moment," it would certainly not be an idealistic portrayal but could just as easily allude to the possibility that Arafat may be leading the Palestinians into a suicide pact, like Ahab leads the crew of Pequot. For this reason, the same question asked of Ahab could also be asked concerning Arafat: "What is he doing when he lets loose his harpoons of fire and madness?"[21] Perhaps, in reply to this question, as Deleuze writes in 1989: *"He is breaking a pact . . . he is putting his crew in mortal danger."*[22]

Let us now return to the "Treatise on Nomadology," where this suicidal tendency is specifically ascribed to the figure of Kleist's Michael Kolhaas, who invents a war machine that sets itself against the state apparatus in "a struggle that appears to be lost from the start."[23] The example is used throughout their analysis to illustrate one of the two poles in which the war machine tends when it takes war *(pólemos)* as a direct object rather than as what they call a "supplementary" or "synthetic" object. Moreover, it is precisely the problem introduced by this first kind of war machine that breaks with "the imperial order of alliances and armies," which often risks turning against itself according to the first pole, which motivates their entire discussion of the war machine. The question they ask in response is not the same as the refrain of Marxist criticism—that is, "why do all revolutions fail?"—but rather, why are the war machines created as a condition of any "revolutionary becoming" most often those that tend toward the destructive pole and at an extreme point toward "a line of destruction prolonging to the limits of the universe"—that is, "Total war"?[24] Why, in other words, does this particular kind of war machine so often lead directly to suicide and "to the double suicide machine of a solitary man and a solitary woman"?[25] By contrast, the other pole they define as creative, when war is only the means for the creation of something else, which they name "new nonorganic social relations." It is according to the second pole that they explicitly link the figures of popular revolt, revolutionary war, minority warfare, and guerilla warfare, which they claim are *"in conformity with the essence"* of the war machine. This would imply, however, that the other pole, the one that takes "total war" as its object, is *per accidens* (as the Schools would say). In other words, war is not an essential attribute of the war machine, even though it may be the most common one, historically speaking, because the war machine has "displayed from the beginning all the ambiguity that caused it to enter into composition with the other pole [i.e., destruction], and swing toward it from the start."[26]

It is in this last statement, I believe, that we have revealed the entire problematic that motivates Deleuze and Guattari's analysis of the war machine, which explains why they seek to go back to the beginning, prior to the moment when one pole is chosen over another—that is, before the state apparatus is erected and, in order to shield itself against the violence of the war machine it has appropriated as its own supplemental organ, must assign to the latter an object that is external to its

own organs. In what might appear as a blatantly contradictory assertion, *in the end they even claim that the personality of the state enjoys no
"natural" affiliation with the idea of war.* As they write, "States were not
the first to make war; war, of course, is not a phenomenon one finds in
the universality of Nature, as nonspecific violence."[27] In other words,
there is no such thing as "an original State of War in Nature" (i.e., "unspe-
cific violence"); all violence is specific in that it is invented to have an
aim (technologically, ideologically, politically, economically, etc.). This
is the same principle expressed in the invention of weaponry, which
underscores the emphasis Deleuze and Guattari place on the assertion
that the war machine is "invented" and not natural: "We thought it possible to assign the invention of the war machine to the nomads. This
was done only in the historical interest of demonstrating that the war
machine as such was invented."[28] Therefore, after establishing the specific origins of the relationships between the nomadic war machines
and the state-form, they ask, who, then, is ultimately responsible for
creating war in the first place, the state or the nomads? Deleuze and
Guattari do not attempt to answer this question, which in some ways
can be compared to what Foucault called the "enigma of revolts." However, they do at least offer a partial explanation when they say that this
happens when one pole is mistaken for another: a line of destruction is
often confused for creation, death is sometimes seen as the only means
of escape, or, to echo the final statement made by Ahab himself, *death
is a wall shoved too close to me, and so there is only nothingness beyond!*

And yet, I believe the real problem lies elsewhere, and this explains
why Deleuze and Guattari's concept of the war machine ultimately fails
to distinguish between the two types of violence, expressed according
to the two species of violence described in the beginning of this chapter. Consequently, from the very start Deleuze and Guattari must admit
that "violence is found everywhere, but only under different regimes and
economies."[29] In other words, the real problem, as I have argued earlier
concerning the enemy, is separating violence from violence in the first
instance—that is, in pretending to distinguish purely destructive violence from creative and productive conflict. This was the same problem

for Plato, as we saw, and his solution was also an attempt to distinguish the two poles of violence by causing one to always be directed outward, away from the city, precisely toward the nomadic bands and the "natural enemy" (i.e., the Persian); at the same time, he wanted to preserve creative violence and conflict as a form internal to the social segments in the city and assign to this pole the production of friendship (i.e., "political economy"). Was this simply Plato's error? Was the belief that he could separate and keep separate the two poles of violence, keep them distinguished so that one pole would never be confused with another and keep the objects distinct so that "the friend" would never be mistaken for "enemy," somewhat naïve? (Is this not, as Derrida will later also say of Schmitt, "Plato's Dream")?[30] And yet, is this not the error of all "political economies," including that of Marx? The pretension to distinguish one kind of violence from the other, but most of all, to make violence productive, to put it to work for a higher goal; to cause it to become creative, just, even "pure" and "reasonable" (i.e., rationalized under certain specific conditions, such as *jus belli*). Perhaps no other contemporary philosopher has addressed this power and concerted rationalization better than Derrida when he writes that, on the basis of its historical abuses, "there is essentially no longer anything today that could in all rigor be called war or terrorism, even if there can still be, here and there, in a secondary sense, surviving vestiges of this paradigm" (i.e., the paradigm of foundational or emancipatory violence as a justification of war, or the right of the peoples to wage war as a mean of liberation).[31] Finally, is this not the same paradigm compounded by all the political theories that have spread across the face of the earth, particularly from the West, that have only served to create a worldwide order from the initial chaos of violence that may actually be, in the end, "a peace more terrifying than fascist death"?[32]

But here we might also consider whether Deleuze and Guattari's theory of an image of "revolutionary becoming of a people" merely serves to recapitulate the same species of error on a different plane. After all, do they not also pretend to discern the difference between the two kinds of violence, described throughout, as the difference between the kind of violence effected by a war machine and the kind of violence effected by the state, or between a line of flight that is creative (even if it must sometimes pass through war) versus a line of destruction and domination? But who ultimately decides? Of course, our answer will depend on how we take the objective of their theories concerning these two kinds of violence. In the conclusion, they write: "The question is not one of quantities but of the incommensurable character of the quantities that confront one another in the two kinds of war machine, according to the two poles."[33] According to the earlier statement quoted above, there is one point of view where the difference between the two poles is greatest: death. In other words, it is by inhabiting this perspective that one might introduce a maximal difference in order to separate violence from violence, in order to cause something to appear. As Deleuze and Guattari speculate, this something = x would have to do with what they call the "incommensurable character of the quantities that confront one another in the two kinds of war machine."[34]

Therefore, in order to occupy the perspective, or "point of view," of death, as if staring out from death's own eyes, one line of research to pursue would be to continue to analyze the conceptual personae that Deleuze and Guattari themselves privilege. Yet there is Ahab, and death is equal to the vision of a white wall and the nothingness beyond. To this image corresponds the specific death produced by one kind of war machine: pure destruction, extermination, and genocidal extinction. "Nothingness, Nothingness!"[35] Historically speaking, human societies have created a dizzying number of manners of producing death. It is in this area that our species is exceptionally creative—*much more so than prodigious nature herself,* as Kant might say. For example, Albert Camus, who once said that if one has difficultly imagining the death caused by a plague, one only has to think of an audience in a movie theater being piled up in the town square. And yet, nowadays such quantities are not so difficult to imagine, are they? Moreover, through the technological development of late-capitalist societies, we have created a kind of death that is aimed at entire populations. This is the death created by the technological advancement of the war machine of the first kind: total extermination, absolute extinction, and the production of nearly infinite quantities along a scale that corresponds to final-stage universal capitalism. In the final pages of their 1984 treatise, Deleuze and Guattari already forecast the development of worldwide total war against an "unspecified enemy" as the final stage in the development of the war machine appropriated by globalized capitalist societies, which they posit as the second, postfascist figure of a war machine that poses "the peace of Terror or Survival" as an absolute decision. As they write:

> Doubtless, the present situation is highly discouraging. We have watched the war machine grow stronger and stronger, as in a science fiction story; we have seen it assign as its objective a peace that is more terrifying than fascist death; we have seen it maintain or instigate the most terrible local wars as parts of itself; we have seen it set sights on a new type of enemy, no longer another State, nor even another regime, but the "unspecified enemy."[36]

Yet Deleuze and Guattari will also speak of a more rare kind of death that aims for something positive (an object) beyond the wall, thus making use of death as a pure transition or *becoming*. And yet, what images do they use to represent this second kind of death? The guerilla fighter? The minority? Clearly, it seems that today we lack a distinctive image for this second point of view. Maybe this is because the death produced by the second kind of war machine, according to the second pole (the creative one), is too populous and is animated by a different character of quantity that directly confronts the death of the first kind, according to the first pole? It goes without saying that there can be small bands of minorities, and minorities of minorities, who can join together in fewer quantities, and necessarily so, and these groups may also constitute new nonorganic social relations. But is our only hope to become survivors and refugees of a "total war against an unspecified enemy" produced by a war machine that today covers the entire surface of the earth?[37] Perhaps it is for this reason that Deleuze and Guattari admit, even twenty years before 9/11 and the "worldwide war on terror," that "the present situation is highly discouraging," since the war machine has grown like a creature in science fiction, "has taken charge of the aim, world-wide order, and the States are now [even then] no more than objects or means adapted to that machine."[38]

To conclude—and here I am only speculating—perhaps the point of view of this second kind of death, according to the second pole, would be a purely impersonal one. Here I am thinking of the scene from a story by Charles Dickens that appears in Deleuze's final meditation written shortly before his own suicide, concerning a character who is first described as "supple to the twist and turn as a Rogue has ever been," someone who was not even liked that much as an individual but whose moment of approaching death occasioned in everyone who witnessed this moment something resembling "a feeling of beatitude."[39] In other words, perhaps all the contemporary philosopher would have to do is open his or her eyes again to see that often *the most common and ordinary death can offer us the greatest occasions for resistance*. That is, only if we choose to see it. Does this secret of a common death refer to an event only meant to be shared between friends, between members of the family, or can it be shared with others, including strangers as well? Has it not been philosophy's highest task to become equal to this image of a purely impersonal life (and thus of a purely common death) in order to provide an adequate concept that would also be the basis for the creation of new nonorganic social relations? Could this image become revolutionary or "political" under certain definite conditions, especially when the real possibilities of either transformative politics or real revolution seem to be lacking today? To quote a line from Jeremy Bentham that also serves as the epigraph to this study: "Let it not be objected that the age is not ripe for such a proposal: the more it wants of being ripe, the sooner we should begin *to do what can be done to ripen it; the more we should do to ripen it. A proposal of this sort, is one of those things that can never come too early nor too late.*"

Conclusion

Toward a Peaceful Confederacy?
(Lat. *foidus pacificum*)

> The world community—this rational idea of a peaceful, albeit not friendly, universal community of all nations on earth that can come into mutual active relations with one another is not a philanthropic (ethical) principle, but rather a juridical principle.
>
> —Immanuel Kant, *Metaphysical Elements of Justice*

According to Kant's late work on the *Principles of Politics* (1793), the irreducible problem of the human species is the following: the human being is an animal and thus, to live peacefully with other animals of its kind, absolutely needs a master. However, this first proposition is immediately compounded by a second: "But this master is an animal too, and thus also requires a master" *(ad infinitum).*[1] Here, in what could be called a regressive hypothesis, Kant establishes the original image of the sovereign as an animal who becomes a master or despot to himself.[2] However, the specific form of animality that Kant refers to in this passage is the *zoon politikon,* since not all animals need masters; therefore, the specific form of animality that Kant has in mind to represent the human species is a domesticated animal. The master, the sovereign, is therefore an exceptional form of animality that belongs only to man, since man is an animal who domesticates himself through the production of his own

137

sovereignty: "Where does man obtain this master? Nowhere but in the Human Race."[3] In other words, as Derrida has also argued, the "beast *and* the sovereign" are exceptions produced by a singular relation to freedom and to law, which can be said to be proper—or, rather, "peculiar" *(idion)*—only *to the animal that "I AM."*[4]

This very paradox also constitutes the internal structure of the "state of exception" in the concept of sovereignty that we also find in Schmitt and Agamben but which is ultimately derived from the philosophy of Thomas Hobbes and is based on an extreme form of logical contradiction that is also found to be internal to the principle of sovereign right. At the same time, in the opening of the second part of his exposition, Kant clarifies that there is a logical need for the principle of the exception and resolves this contradiction (which actually pertains to the concept of equality) in the following manner. He writes:

> The Sovereign or Supreme Ruler of the State is excepted, because he is regarded not as a mere Member of the Commonwealth, but as its Creator or Maintainer; and he alone has the Right to compel without being himself subject to compulsory Law. All, however, who live under Laws in a State, are its subjects; and, consequently, they are subjected to the compulsory Law, like all other members of the Commonwealth, one only, *whether an individual Sovereign or a collective body,* constituting the Supreme Head of the State, and as such being accepted as the medium through which alone all rightful coercion or compulsion can be exercised. For, should the Head of the State also be subject to compulsion, there would no longer be a Supreme Head, *and the series of members subordinate and superordinate would go on upwards ad infinitum.* Again, were there in the State two such powers as persons exempt from legal compulsion, neither of them would be subject to compulsory Laws, and as such the one could do no wrong to the other; which is impossible.[5]

What Kant describes in the above is, in fact, precisely the relation between two or more sovereign individuals of the nation-state, each of which appeal to their own right in a state of anarchy and freedom to go to war to protect their own right and, thus, continue to dwell in a state of nature, which is equivalent to the "concrete situation" of war. In the eighteenth-century arena of international relations determined by the right of nations, nations cannot be compelled or coerced to submit to the right of another state except through violence and war. As stated in the second definitive principle of his treatise *Toward Perpetual Peace,* written two years later, in 1795, Kant is clearly aware that he is stating a blatant contradiction in the concept of right that is embodied in the historical nation-state of his time. (I return to this below in great detail.) Therefore, as a rational principle, this notion of right is immediately unfounded as contradictory and illogical—the idea of political right as a form of reason that is not consistent with its own principle. Because it remains in an ontological state of being ungrounded, it is open to illegitimate and arbitrary appropriation by whatever form of sovereignty that appears to subtract its own right from this infinite movement of subordination and superordination that is first of all caused by the lack of proper foundation of the law itself—that is, the very principle of right— and it is this exception that allows this being (whether an individual or a collective of individuals) to appear as if *above the law.*

Although Kant's explanation of the sovereign state of exception appears to echo—or, more accurately, to prefigure—the explanation given by Schmitt (on whom Agamben depends for his own argument), for Kant, this is merely the natural condition of law, the principle from which neither Schmitt nor Agamben ever seem to depart, but not what he calls its "supernatural destination," which is not to be reduced to the image of transcendence that the sovereign individual gives to himself (or even that "a people" give to themselves) by invoking a state of exception. In fact, the idea of a "supernatural destiny" does not immediately lead to a theological concept of sovereignty, although it might serve as the basis for a critique of the imperfect conception of sovereignty at the basis of both politics and religion, whether in the despotic or pastoral images of the sovereign as prince or God the father; in the revolutionary image of a people as the foundational basis of the nation; or, finally, even in the image of humanity itself. As Derrida also argues, it is precisely this lack of a proper foundation of law that will allow the principle of sovereign right to become self-critical, which is to say, contradictory, as when two claims of sovereignty confront each other and this conflict cannot be resolved by any recourse to positive law, as in the case of any universal claim to human rights.

In the passage that follows the definition of the form of sovereignty that is distinctive (or peculiar) to the human species, Kant goes on to speculate that there are other extraterrestrial species in the universe who have solved this dilemma of sovereignty, and "it may be the case that in those other planets every individual attains his destination in life, but with us it is otherwise, since we can only hope for this [destination] as a species."[6] Therefore, as he states elsewhere, it is only through the political constitution that the human species will be able to finally "work out" the eternal riddle of sovereignty, but this is a riddle or problem that can only be worked out as one species, and can never be resolved by multiple forms of sovereignty (individual or collective), which in Kant's time would refer to the conflicting sovereignties of the nation-states but also, in the same moment, to the multiplication of races and peoples, since this would only refer again to a state of nature where two (or more) sovereign individuals confront each other "and neither would be subject to compulsory law, and as such neither could do any wrong to the other, which is impossible," as Kant states above. And yet, this is a reformulation of the state of nature in Hobbes, which Kant defines as the state of war that actually defines the present moment and not some mythical past prior to the emergence of the idea of civil society and primarily in those vast and open spaces that exist between nations where there is no law (deserts, arctic wastelands, oceans, etc.) and thus no basis for any claim or recourse to justice as well. As Kant writes, "In this condition the Human Race will remain until it shall have worked itself . . . out of the existing chaos of its political relations."[7]

Therefore, while the principle of sovereignty appears first in the natural order that codetermines the distinguishing and exceptional (and peculiar) characteristic of the animal that is man, the true principle of politics itself appears as the last to be practically worked completely through *(durcharbeiten)* for the entire human species (ironically echoing Marx's later formulation of "a determination in the last instance"). Here, the term "worked out" *(abverdiene)* refers to the material and the corresponding knowledge (skill, or *techne*) that is exemplified by an artist who knows how to shape the material into a perfect form. In this case, as Kant says later, since "man is a crooked material that cannot be bent into a straight line," the artist is nature *(natura daedala rerum)* who bends the material of man to her own design. Essentially, Kant revises the relationship between *natural origin* and *historical end (Zweck)* to support the argument that while law has a natural origin, it has a supernatural destination. In other words, the idea of sovereignty has a natural beginning (i.e., the sovereign is an animal who becomes a master) but a supernatural destination according to the idea of Providence (i.e., the "cosmo-political design of Nature") that is sketched at the end of *Principles of Politics.*[8] At the end of the eighteenth century, Kant locates the progress of our species as being located somewhere at a middle rung of perpetual progress; however, judging from the political events of the past two centuries, we might wonder if our species has fallen more than a few rungs on the ladder of perpetual progress—that is, if our species has not fallen off the ladder entirely. But already in view of the situation of colonialism even in Kant's own time, which he completely anathematizes in *Toward Perpetual Peace* and other political writings of the last period,[9] the ladder is very high and already appears impossible to climb, despite the fact there are some corners of the world where human beings enjoy a relative measure of rest and security—recalling the argument of the previous section, these relatively "peaceful" enclosures of humanity are fast becoming disproportionate to the "real hell in which most of the human population lives today."[10]

Is there not a way of understanding what Kant is referring to as the "supernatural destination" of the human species as in some way related to Antelme's own conscious certainty of the unity of the human species on the basis of his experience as a deportee and as a survivor of the camps in response to the SS fantasy that "it was their historical mission to change species, and when the mutation was happening too slowly, to kill"?[11] As he writes:

> For in fact everything happens in that world [that is, of that fantasy] as though there were a number of species, or, rather, *as though belonging to a single species wasn't certain,* as though you could join the species or leave it, could be halfway in or belong to it fully, or never belong to it, try as you might for generations, divisions into races and classes being the canon of the species and sustaining the axiom that we're always prepared to use as our ultimate line of defense: "They aren't people like us."[12]

Contrary to most of the political and moral philosophy that has been written in the post-war period, the condition of this certainty would also disqualify any moral pretension that the SS were also not people like us; rather, "the SS are only men like ourselves."

> If, at the moment when the distance between beings is at its greatest, at the moment when the subjugation of some and the power of others have attained such limits as to seem frozen into some supernatural distinction; if facing nature, or facing death, we can perceive no substantial difference between the SS and ourselves, then we have to say that there is only one human race.[13]

Consequently, like Antelme's negative conception of friendship, for Kant, the idea of humanity may have no positive (i.e., moral) value but remains the name of that proper impossibility that belongs to the idea of the political, which is to say, of a final (cosmo)political constitution of the human species.

> Begin, then, as he may, it is not easy to see how he can procure a supreme Authority over public justice that would be essentially just, whether such an authority may be sought in a single person or in a society of many selected persons. The highest authority has to be just in itself, and yet to be a man. This problem, is, therefore, the most difficult

of its kind; and, indeed, its perfect solution is impossible. Out of such crooked material as man is made of, nothing can be hammered quite straight. So it is only an approximation to this Idea that is imposed upon us by Nature. It further follows that this problem is the last to be practically worked out, because it requires correct conceptions of the nature of a possible Constitution, great experience founded on the practice of ages, and above all a good will prepared for the reception of the solution. But these three conditions could not easily be found together; and if they are found it can only be very late in time, and after many attempts to solve the problem had been made in vain.[14]

If we seemed to have arrived at a point of impasse in imagining a concept of the political that would be capable of encompassing the entire species—that is, "in the last instance"—this would either become the occasion of abandoning the concept of politics altogether (as either impossible or certainly unrealizable) or of affirming this impossibility itself as the most proper impossibility that belongs to the animal that is man. The first option, of course, has already been taken up and justified by a neoliberal principle of society that has surrendered (literally handed over) any political ideal of the unity of the species to the unconscious principle of pure market relations—that is, to an economic determination of man "in the final instance," what Foucault has named *homo economicus*.[15] The second option has been taken up by several contemporary philosophies (Derrida, especially, but also Agamben) that grasp this form of negativity that remains in every sovereign claim to a political principle as a supremely "critical" form of historico-philosophical reflection, one that still remains nonetheless open to the possibility of a "new politics": either one that is no longer founded on the inclusion/exclusion of *zoē* in *bios* but that "remains largely to be invented," according to Agamben's claim,[16] or one that Derrida often invokes as a "democracy to come" *(à venir)* but remains only in the form of a "promise"—and remains despite every negative assertion or evidence to the contrary—yet still remains somehow the "property of man." Of course, there are other options out there as well, which could be categorized as metapolitical concepts such as "the idea of communism" (albeit a communism without politics) or of "absolute democracy" (albeit a democracy without a state). However, from the perspective of a critical philosophy that might still be worthy of the name, these can only be viewed as "transcendental illusions"—that is to say, the most recent failures of our faculties (and the sublime failure of the imagination in particular) to empirically determine the idea of the complete political constitution of the human species.

Returning to the second option, perhaps this is nowhere more eloquently stated than in the following lengthy passage from *The Beast and the Sovereign* on the principle of sovereignty itself:

[If sovereignty is, indeed, defined as the proper of man,] it is nonetheless also in the name of man, the humanity of man, the dignity of man [that is to say, recalling Benveniste's analysis of the institution of hospitality, an appeal to *aidōs*], therefore a certain proper of man, that a certain modernity has begun to question, to undermine, to put into crisis nation-state sovereignty. Every time one refers to the universality of human rights (beyond the rights of man and citizen), every time one invokes the recent concept (1945) of crime against humanity or genocide, in order to implement an international right or even an international penal tribunal, or even humanitarian actions the initiative for which is taken by NGOs (nongovernmental organizations), every time one militates for the universal abolition of the death penalty, etc., then one is calling into question the principle and the authority of the sovereignty of the nation-state, and doing so in the name of man, the right of man, the proper of man. It is in the name of a certain proper of man, which sometimes remains, so I believe, completely to be thought, merely promised to a thought which does not yet think what it thinks it thinks and that the *doxa* accredits with a firmness matched only by its naïveté, it is in the name of a certain supposed proper of man, of the humanity of man, that one limits, delimits, and circumscribes, even beats back, combats, and denounces the sovereignty of the nation-state. I'm careful to say the sovereignty of the state and the nation-state, for the humanity of man or of the human person invoked by human rights or the concept of crime against humanity, by international right or the international penal agencies—all these agencies might well be invoking another sovereignty, the sovereignty of man himself, of the very being of man himself *(ipse, ipsissimus)* above and beyond and before state or nation-state sovereignty.[17]

Here we have the eternal claim of a higher sovereignty, humanity, that nevertheless remains "promised to a thought which does not yet think what it thinks and that the *doxa* accredits with a firmness matched only by its naïveté"; the claim that "the highest authority has to be just in itself, and yet to be a man."[18] In this regard, Derrida seems to agree with Kant—and this is the entire basis of his long argument with Schmitt (who I have called the natural lawyer of our time)—that the mastery or sovereignty that is proper to man is not the natural sovereignty of he who decides the state of exception but rather it refers to the possibility of an infinite superordination of the principle of sovereignty that will prove, in turn, to unfound any claim by a historical representative, thus opening it to an intense questioning. And yet, this power of questioning is only possible on the condition of a prior refusal to an external "Will," since as Kant writes, "there can be nothing more dreadful than that the actions of one person are placed under the Will of another."[19] Recalling the statement by Antelme, this is another sovereign power that is first expressed by the conscious refusal of the order of a master—that is, the right to say no or, according to the Kantian phrase, "the right of Humanity in our own Person" *(der Menschen)*. As an expression of its transcendental condition, however, this right can have no proper foundation in any positive law.

At this point, however, we must be careful not to lapse into yet another moral philosophy extolling the peaceful image of humanity, since this freedom from any positive order of law (whether just or unjust) that lies at the origin of the sovereign claim of exception also makes possible the power to refuse this order in the name of another form of sovereignty (e.g., in the name of humanity itself). In other words, it is the same principle of right that is led into a violent contradiction when two (or more) sovereign claims confront each other in absolute opposition. In such a case, neither claim can even be said to be "equal," since this would presuppose a third principle of universality under which both claims could be measured—once again, a principle of right or justice guaranteed by the rule of law. Throughout this study I have evoked the two sovereign figures of the global rich and poor to refer to a "concrete situation" of war today, one that is being waged today outside any political constitution of government or juridical constitution of right, in the "war-zones" that grow and multiply each day: in the deserts that lie between the territorial nation-states and also within the global urban slums and the barrios south of the border or within the vast flows of human capital that exist virtually in the interstitial spaces of *commercium*. Again, recalling Antelme's conclusion, today, the rich man can no longer be redeemed by his image of politics, and the poor man can no longer be justified by his image of sacredness. Both cloaks have been stripped away and the two sovereign figures of humanity that lie beneath have revealed themselves to be pure beasts, and there are no oaths *(hórkia)* between beasts, and thus no possible claim to the right of hospitality *(aidōs),* recalling the line from Homer's Achilles:

> Do not propose an agreement. There are no pledges *(hórkia pistá)* between lions and men. The hearts of wolves and sheep do not beat in unison, but constantly do they devise evil for each other; "even so is it not possible for you and me to be in *philótēs,* and there will be no *hórkia* between us": *emè kaì sè philēmenai oudé ti nōin hórkia éssontai* (until one or the other is killed).[20]

It is in this "concrete situation" of war that an ever-growing demographic portion of humanity lives today, where there is neither rule of law nor any possibility of justice but rather an essential lawless field of battle, since neither claim can be founded on any principle of universal right, which is to say, *neither in the name of humanity nor in the name of the prophet.*

Derrida has addressed this worsening situation elsewhere under the term "globalatinization," where he writes:

> The task, therefore, seems all the more urgent and problematic (incalculable calculation of religion for our times) as the demographic disproportion will not cease henceforth to threaten external hegemony, leaving the latter no other stratagem other than internalization.[21]

Here, in other words, we are reminded of the strength of Schmitt's accusation against the concept of humanity *(Menschheit)* as only the most cunning and hegemonic of modern concepts—like a wolf in sheep's clothing—to be responsible for the modern neutralization of the political concept "in its purity"—that is, for the "depoliticization" *(Entpolitisierung)* of genuine state interests, which has proven to be especially useful as a technical instrument for the imperialist expansion or simply as a "ruse of war."[22] Of course, Schmitt is absolutely correct, and Kant says as much also—that, empirically speaking, humanity is more of a devil than an angel—but the conceptual personage of the rogue *(Schelm)* is exclusively reserved for the race of masters who appear to claim the state of sovereign exception. For example, at the very same moment he was making this critique, Schmitt himself was in the process of expounding on the Nuremburg Laws, which he called "the constitution of freedom," and adjudicating those Nazi racial concepts that could be applied to current case law, since "the legislation provides for the protection and the *purity* [here again, this word, and is there any wonder why Derrida absolutely detests its use in Schmitt?] of *volkish* blood."[23]

Let us now return to the theme of impossibility, this time from a practical point of view. Actually, for Kant there are three distinct impossibilities, each of which corresponds to an idea of pure reason: the impossibility of eternal peace, the impossibility of universal friendship (or consensus of minds), and the impossibility of a universal political constitution of humanity under a common principle of law. Such a constitution can appear only as a regulative idea of a cosmopolitical constitution of man—that is, as the fourth idea of pure reason, which Kant later adds to the ideas that appear in the *Critique of Pure Reason*: God, world, and soul. For Kant, once again, humanity is a species that lies somewhere between animality and personality (or psychology), the latter of which is informed by the diversity of culture, geography, history, and political constitution. In each of these cases, Kant claims, the idea allows us to represent (problematically) the systematic unity toward which we aspire and that we presuppose in empirical studies or in practice. Again, unreal is taken here in a special sense of having a purely theoretical appearance (i.e., the soul cannot be empirically proven and the world cannot be viewed in one glance). For example, in accordance with the idea of God, we "consider every connection in the world according to principles *[Principien]* of a systematic unity, hence *as if* they had all arisen from one single all-encompassing being, as supreme and all-sufficient cause."[24] Of course, some might argue that the idea of God already contains the maximal extension of the concept of community and the idea of the soul the maximal intention of the concept of subjectivity (or psychology), but it is only the idea of politics that contains the maximal extension, over time, of the principle of right, law, or justice, and the concept of free will.

Impossible! Impossible!! Impossible!!! Given these three impossibilities, as he argues in *Toward Perpetual Peace,* the best "we" can hope for is a negative approximation of each idea in the form of a surrogate that at least preserves the idea until such time that a future race might finally have the knowledge, experience, and skill to "work it out" in practice. First, as a surrogate for an actual state of peace, it is perhaps only in the late philosophy of Kant that a notion of "peace" first emerges that is stripped of its earlier religious and cultural associations, as well as a relationship between strangers that is stripped of the sentimentality of friendship. Instead, Kant defines the concept of peace as the purely juridical character of a legal relationship between strangers that is not necessarily linked to an ethical or affective notion of friendship. This conception is stated in the first proposition that defines the nature and conditions of "Cosmo-political Right" *(jus cosmipoliticum),* where he defines "the rational idea of a peaceful, if not a friendly, universal community of all the Nations upon the earth that may come into active relations with each other, that is, a juridical principle, as distinguished from philanthropic or ethical principles."[25] In other words, contrary to all the misgivings held concerning the philosopher of Königsberg, even by dint of a sleepwalker, Kant recovered one of the original institutions of friendship (or hospitality) by founding the concept of political right neither on the private individual nor on the natural subject of the citizen of the nation but rather on the being of the stranger who we have argued throughout is determined strictly by statutory terms, meaning in Kant's time as well as our own, since the term "peace" is strictly determined according to the rights of strangers under the principle of international law.

Second, as the negative surrogate for the idea of a complete political constitution of the human race (what some commentators have identified as Kant's idea of a world government but usually according to the historical image of the totalitarian state), Kant proposes the "establishment of a surrogate" in the "Confederacy of Peace" *(foidus pacificum)*, which later becomes the basic framework for the League of Nations. In the second definitive article, immediately preceding the article of universal hospitality, Kant specifically foresees the establishment of "an ever-growing STATE OF NATIONS, such as would at last embrace all of the Nations of the Earth." But then he immediately goes on to outline the conditions of its failure:

> But as the Nations, according to their ideas of international Right, will not have such a positive rational system, and consequently reject in fact *(in thesi)* what is right in theory *(in hypothesi)*, it cannot be realized in this pure form. Hence, instead of the positive idea of a Universal Republic—if all is not to be lost—we shall have as result only the negative surrogate of a Federation of the States averting war, subsisting in an external union, and always extending itself over the world.[26]

However, Kant already predicts the failure of this surrogate in 1795 as he outlines the imperfections in international law in his own time—so now we have a fourth impossibility! The accuracy with which Kant predicts the failure of the current United Nations is equally uncanny and remarkable, which leads us immediately to Kant's basic argument: in order for a positive system of international law to be established, first we must transform the concept of national right and, in particular, the rights of war *(jus belli)*.

Before proceeding to this argument, however, let's turn to read the first article, which outlines a practice that can be immediately prohibited by a strict conception of right *(leges strictae):* "No treaty of peace shall be regarded as valid, if made with the secret reservation of material for a future war."[27] A peace treaty *(Freidensvertrag, pactum pacis)* is regarded merely as a provisional instrument, or a contract between two or more parties, for ending current hostilities. Parties may enter into a contract with certain moral or practical reservations that they choose to hold in secret, first of all, because the nature of a contract is that it is always provisional and temporary, subject to changing circumstances outside the control and knowledge of the original framers, but more importantly, because no contract can become binding for all eternity without itself becoming a source of injustice for future peoples who were not party to the original agreement, as has often happened. Nevertheless, as Kant writes elsewhere, all legal treaties are endowed with an air of being sacred scripture, and it is the peculiarity of this instrument that protects it—and the participants—from falling into a state of blatant hypocrisy. Throughout the arguments of *Toward Perpetual Peace,* Kant often makes a distinction between the provisional state of peace occasioned by a treaty and a more permanent state of peace (as something approximating "eternal peace" on this earth and among human agents) that could only be brought about by the creation of a federation of free states, or by a "League of Peace" *(feodus pacificum).*

Practical or moral reservations aside, however, no treaty can be regarded as legally valid *(gelten)* in cases where one or more parties willingly and consciously enter into a sacred oath for peace all the while reserving the material *(Stoffe)* for future war. Here, the argument is based on the first principle of contract law: no contract can be held as valid (i.e., legal) if its very terms are self-contradictory so as to cancel each other out. There is also a logical, practical, and moral argument as well: logically speaking, a treaty that reserves the material for war is merely a truce; practically speaking, the treaty itself would be classified as material, since its secret reservation would be used as the very cause for resuming the war; and morally, the "practical politicians "who craft such a duplicitous and publically misleading device" are accused in the gloss on the article of "Jesuitical casuistry" and of acting beneath the dignity of their public offices. Nevertheless, immediately following this moral argument there is the clause "If one judges the facts as they really are," and here Kant is implicitly referring to actual persons of the state and historical treaties, even though the reference is oblique because Kant was already placed under an imperial censorship for his previous writings on religion a year earlier. In fact, the clause refers to the historical sovereigns of Fredrick the Great (1740–86) and his successor Fredrick Wilhelm II (1786–97), as well as to an actual incident where, after invading Silesia, Fredrick II engaged a certain "duplicitous minister" who crafted a treaty that he later praised for its duplicitousness as "the work of an excellent charlatan."[28] Kant himself likely had this treaty in mind when he referred to treaties that reserve material for future war, as well as to the "Jesuit casuistry" of those warmongering despots and rogues who "with indifference leave the justification of the war, for the sake of propriety, to the diplomatic corps, which is always ready to provide it."[29] However, the most severe condemnation comes later on in his version of the famous *fiat justitia et pereat mundus* against the perpetrators of "radical evil": "Let righteousness prevail though all the rogues *(Schelme)* in the world should perish for it."[30]

Turning now to the second definitive article, the historical and dramatic irony of this historical situation is nowhere more present than in the arguments against those Kant refers to as "the miserable comforters" *(leidege Troster),* here evoking the situation of Job before the empty consolations of his so-called friends. According to the legal theorist Georg Cavallar, the objects of Kant's scorn (and the fictional representatives of Job's coterie of false friends) are Hugo Grotius, Samuel von Pufendorf, and Emer de Vattel (henceforth called "the natural lawyers") who defend—or at least accept as inevitable and in principle—the just right of nations to go to war *(jus belli).*[31] Against the principles of what he regards as a "weak cosmopolitanism" that is eviscerated by the current notion of national right, Kant writes:

> The depravity of human nature is exhibited without disguise in the unrestrained relations of the Nations to each other, whereas in the legalized state of Civil Society it is greatly veiled under the constraint of government. In view of it, we may well wonder that the word "Right" has not yet been entirely banished from the policy of war as pedantic, and that no State has as yet ventured to declare itself publicly in favor of that doctrine. For Grotius, Pufendorf, Vattel and the others—*miserable comforters all of them!*—are still always quoted cordially for the justification of an outbreak of war, although their philosophically or diplomatically composed codes have not, nor could have, the slightest legal force, since the States as such stand under no common legal constraint; and there is not an example of a State having been ever moved to desist from its purpose by arguments [i.e., by mere words], although armed with testimonies of such important men.[32]

Before developing Kant's objections to the natural lawyers, let us first recall the situation of Job that is being evoked as a dramatic context for judging the different providential and moral explanations for Job's extreme state of suffering, which is nothing less than the state of being a deportee and survivor of God's cruel war against him. As we all know, Job was the richest man in the East. According to Elie Wiesel's commentary on the *Midrash,* "He was rich, hospitable, friendly and giving; he invited strangers into his home without asking who they were or what the purpose of their visit might be. He welcomed the hungry and helped the poor, angels and beggars alike, offering them both shelter and food."[33] According to his divine accuser, however, Job's virtues were merely the result of the fact that God has "placed a hedge around him, his family, and everything he has" (not unlike the security of the richest populations in the world today). In order to test this thesis, God agrees to allow the accuser to "wage war" on Job and his possessions; Job is stripped of everything and his children are put under the sword. Even his wife pleads with him to forgo his insane claim of innocence, "to curse God, and die!" At this point, Job's three friends appear to mourn with Job and to comfort him; however, like the friends of Antelme, "when they arrived and saw Job from a distance, they could barely recognize him."[34]

After seven days and nights when the group of friends sat together in dust and silence, finally the friends began speaking of Job's situation. In the various arguments put forth, all Job's friends raise in light of Job's intolerable situation that God's war against him must have been "just." In response, Job refuses to relinquish his innocence before this supposed judgment of God and instead charges God with committing an injustice against him with his sovereign decision, and thus the discourses that ensue constitute a trial against God's order, with Job now in the position of the accused and the friends quickly changing sides to appear as his prosecutors (just as friends often are the first to do in a time of distress). In his own defense, Job often describes "the voice from the whirlwind" (the sovereign) as a predatory animal, a lion that hunts him down and chews his flesh: "In his rage he hunted and caught me; he cracked my bones in his teeth. I was whole—he ripped me apart, chewed my body to pulp." In the end, "the voice from the whirlwind" is revealed only as a God of nature, of storms and earthquakes, "king over all the proud beasts" equal to none, who speaks of his secret design, which Job's accusers only smear with darkness, even though the voice will also confirm that all of Job's accusations are true. At one point in the dialogue, Job even suggests that he is the victim of mistaken identity, of "friendly fire, and that God had simply mistaken the name of Job (*Iyov*) for the Hebrew name of enemy (*Oyev*)."

In the beginning of the second monologue, the voice protests: "I don't confuse moments, or lightning bolts, or drops, or roots—and you are asking Me if I am confusing *Iyov* and *Oyev*, Job and Enemy!"[35] Most importantly, the voice admits that treating Job as an enemy was unjust:

"Am I wrong simply because you are right?" It is at this point that in response to the voice, Job chooses to remain silent, but this is neither the silence of piety or submission (as it has been interpreted by religious commentators) but rather the special claim to the right to immunity, the right to silence, which belongs to a special class of immunity, *nemo tenetur se ipsum accusare* (no man is bound to accuse himself), a subspecies of the sovereign right of exception. Moreover, Job's silence can only be understood according to this right, especially given that the entire drama is framed within a legal–juridical context of a trial and even of a higher court of appeal that will hear Job's case between mortals and this lower God at some later date; as Job cries, "Someday my witness would come; my avenger would read those words. He would plead for me in God's court; he would stand up and vindicate my name." Therefore, Job chooses to remain silent rather than to continue to plead his case before a lower court and thus refuses to incriminate himself before the law of a master who is merely an animal, of "the sovereign who is also a beast" (Derrida), and thus whose concept of right cannot be founded on any principle of justice.

I will not go further into all the arguments between Job and his "miserable comforters" and "false friends" that rehearse the different cosmological arguments that belong to this rich legal drama but instead I will return to Kant's allegorical use of Job's situation to illustrate his own arguments against the natural lawyers of his own time. The most damning criticism is that, like Job's friends, the natural lawyers only respond to Job's cry for the dignity and respect (*aidōs*) of the victims by offering "mere arguments" and thus are implicitly responsible for the evil of Job's situation by attempting to rationalize and thus to justify war. In other words, since war is a state of nature, there is no possible justice and, thus, no possible wrong; moreover, by justifying war one must ignore the state of injustice and the real suffering it causes to those who find themselves suddenly outside the hedges, deprived of all political rights. However, the one thing that the natural lawyers never question is the preemptory state of war itself, as a state that society would one day depart, but rather assume it is conclusive and thus a permanent condition of the sovereign right of nations. That is to say, "war is simply politics by other means." According to Cavallar, while "the natural lawyers tend to paint a rosy picture of the state of nature, or international anarchy, for Kant this is a condition of permanent war, and he scolds the lawyers because they do not think it necessary to overcome this condition."[36] It is for this reason that Kant prefers Hobbes's description over their own or even the moral outrage of Jean-Jacques Rousseau with his scenes of war, death, and agony, of ten thousand butchered men and the dead stacked in piles like cords of wood.

Just as at the end of the story of Job, where one man appears as superior to the sovereign, who is merely an animal or a ruler of animals in a state of nature and whose order has been shown to be lawless and arbitrary, lacking any principle of right except that which is grounded on a superior force ("might makes right"), so Kant also refuses that the right of war can in any way be justified by the principle of reason, either now or in the future. Hence:

> The notion of a Right to go to war, cannot be properly conceived as an element in the Right of Nations. For it would be equivalent to a Right to determine what is just not by universal external laws limiting the freedom of every individual alike, but through one-sided maxims that operate by means of force. *If such a Right be conceivable at all it would amount, in fact, to this: that in the case of men who are so disposed it is quite right for them to destroy and devour each other, and thus to find Perpetual Peace only in the wide grave which is to cover all the abomination of the deeds of violence and their authors!* For States viewed in relation to each other, there can be only one way, according to reason, of emerging from that lawless condition which contains nothing but occasions of war.[37]

In response, Kant endorses "neither just war nor lawful war in due form, but juridical cosmopolitanism."[38] There can be no justice through war or during a state of war, which is a contradiction in terms, and thus no rightful concept of "just war." In order to finally quit a state of nature, therefore, one must gradually remove all legal–juridical grounds as well as ethico-moral justifications for the right to war, including the idea of "just war." At the same time, of course, Kant was also a pragmatist, so the gradual process of the creation of international laws that will interdict the nation-state's right of war will take some time, perhaps even centuries, but will gradually arrive at a state approximating perpetual peace.

The moral or political irony of this situation is set forth in the secret article contained in the second supplement, which can be regarded as a third surrogate for the idea of peace (*pax*). It is thus detached from the main body of the public treatise that outlines the preliminary and definitive articles and rather offered as a secret pact. It reads: "The maxims of the philosophers regarding the conditions of the possibility of a public peace shall be taken into consideration by the States that are armed for war."[39] The reason for this secret article is that it may not be compatible with the dignity of certain persons to publicly acknowledge the origins of the idea of perpetual peace. The person to whom Kant refers is, however, not himself, since the philosopher is nowhere capable of dictating anything into law, but rather the contemporary statesmen and "practical politician" (the natural lawyer), who unfortunately holds the very idea with such contempt that they would never claim to be associated with it, much less acknowledge that perpetual peace is an idea first originated with him—that is, as the final "end" (*Zweck*) of politics and law. Therefore, "it can be said that the establishment of a universal and enduring peace is not just a part, but rather constitutes the whole, of the ultimate purpose of justice and Law (*Rechtslehre*) within the bounds of pure reason."[40] At the same time, however, since the ultimate purpose of perpetual peace is to serve as the practical idea of law, it must be disguised as theoretical and speculative and assigned to the philosopher only due to the statesman's limitations (lack of experience, technical knowledge, and artistic skill according to the three conditions named earlier) for realizing this idea in human affairs. The philosopher thus functions merely as a historical surrogate, one whose purpose is to preserve the idea of perpetual peace by its secret cloak of its impossibility to realize in the present moment.

As Kant writes toward the conclusion of the *Rechtslehre* published two years after *Toward Perpetual Peace*: "If one cannot prove that a thing is, he may try to prove that it is not. And if he succeeds in doing neither (as is often the case), he may still ask whether it is in his interest to accept one alternative over the over hypothetically, from the theoretical or practical point of view."[41] As in his earlier response to Mendelssohn, Kant chooses the more positive hypothesis even though it can't actually be proven—but then, as Kant observes, it cannot be disproven either and thus still remains an a priori idea of Reason. This remains a crucial point for Kant's critical philosophy as well as his revision of the relationship between theory and practice, or theoretical and practical knowledge. Accordingly, concerning the idea of perpetual peace,

> there is no longer any question as to whether perpetual peace is a reality or a fiction and whether we deceive ourselves if we assume in a theoretical judgment that it is real. We must, however, act as though perpetual peace were a reality, which perhaps it is not, by working for its establishment and for the kind of constitution that seems best adapted to bringing it about (perhaps some form of republicanism in every state), in order to bring perpetual peace and an end to the abominable practice of war, which up to now has been the chief purpose for which every state, without exception, has adapted its institutions. Even if the realization of this goal of abolishing war were to remain just a pious wish, we still would not be deceiving ourselves by adopting the maxim of working for it with unrelenting perseverance.[42]

Moreover, and this is perhaps the crucial point, to choose the other alternative would simply amount to condemning humanity to live in a permanent state of war and thus we would be compelled to agree with the natural lawyers that the idea of peace is merely a "sweet dream" of the philosophers, since the only peace to which "men in general" are destined as a species is the peace of the grave, a sentiment of fate that is echoed in the opening of *Toward Perpetual Peace,* where we have the satirical Dutch Innkeeper's sign on which is painted "*Vrede Eeuwige,*" underneath the image of a graveyard.

In conclusion I now summarize the three historical or negative surrogates of perpetual peace, or of a universal political constitution we have discussed above: first, the treaty or compact of peace (*pactum pacis*) as a temporary or negative surrogate for the idea of a perpetual peace; second, the "Confederacy of Peace" (*foidus pacificum*) and later a federation of states (e.g., the League of Nations) as a negative surrogate for the idea of a world constitution; and third, the philosopher himself as a negative surrogate for the statesman—that is, to stand in for the absence of a subject whose duty would be to practically realize these former ideas in the areas of politics and law but that, in the historical limitations of the nation-state in Kant's time (and also in our own!), would actually conflict with the hegemony of state power and thus the empirically determined ends of politics and law (e.g., war, territory, private property, accumulation of wealth, capital, etc.). Under this negative role, the contemporary political philosopher has but one duty, which we have already addressed in the quotation cited above: to act as if perpetual peace were a reality and "in accordance with the Idea of such an end, even if there is not the slightest theoretical probability that it is feasible, *as long as its impossibility cannot be demonstrated either.*"[43] According to the Kantian definition of the duty of philosophy, therefore, the philosopher acts in the interest of pure reason alone (i.e., to preserve the idea of pure reason by giving its concept a maximal extension or intention through an assumption of its reality) rather than according to the empirical interest of morality, politics, or law. Of course this definition of philosophy has been criticized for some time and may not be the most current definition of the duty of philosophy today or the most recent conceptual persona of the philosopher, including the one Deleuze defines as "the friend of the concept."

In fact, there are many competing images of philosophy and the philosopher, both historical and contemporary, many of which are at war with each other over the establishment of a dominant image of thought.

The principle of war is not peculiar to the field of politics alone but also exists in philosophy through a principle of infinite competition, or rivalry of opinions (*doxa*); however, what may be peculiar to modern philosophy, perhaps in contradistinction to the Greek principle, is that modern philosophy has internalized the principle of war (*pólemos*) in order to project its own image of a "deterritorialized earth" and the principles of battle or combat to describe the movement of thought across this terrain in carrying out new sorties against an enemy who turns out to be humanity itself—who must finally be vanquished in the name of a new people and a newly reterritorialized earth created by militant philosophy, or political theology. Thus, as Deleuze and Guattari write, "philosophy is reterritorialized three times: on the Greeks in the past, on the modern democratic state in the present, and on a new people and a new earth in the future. Greeks and democrats are strangely deformed in the mirror of the future."[44] As I have already discussed in the introduction, we can certainly find this image of thought in the philosophies of Nietzsche and Marx as well as in the contemporary philosophies of Alain Badiou and Deleuze. What seems strangely absent from this field of battle, or what has been abdicated as the final goal of thinking, is any possible horizon of consensus, "peaceful accord," or philosophical image of friendship. To paraphrase again the line earlier attributed to Hölderlin, since we have rejected the spirit of friendship that is first necessary for conversation or written exchange, today we find ourselves by our own hand outside thought.

Nevertheless, perhaps only by means of a reverse proof, I would argue that the Kantian image of the philosopher as surrogate continues to determine the subject of contemporary philosophy, and this can be easily demonstrated by referring to the image of an "end of politics " that appears in works of several philosophers, even in the most divergent philosophical systems, such as we find in the works of Agamben, Badiou, Derrida, Deleuze and Guattari, Negri, Jacques Rancière, and certainly Slavoj Žižek, perhaps the most famous of all contemporary philosophers. In each case, whether in their own primary writings or in the commentaries of their disciples, the conceptual personage of the philosopher

continues to function as the negative surrogate of the practical politician, and the most dominant philosophies today are those that relentlessly pursue a "final end" by means of whatever image they choose to
assign this end: an end to sovereignty, an end to politics, an end to
capitalism, an end to democracy and/or totalitarianism, and end to all
forms of racism and "speciesism." *And yet, there is one end that philosophy seems to have fallen strangely silent about, which is the end of war.* It
is for this reason that in this conclusion I continue to privilege the philosophy of Kant, who argued that it is only after we bring about the end
of "the abominable practice of war" that we can even begin to pursue
these other higher goals. Or perhaps it is only in the course of "working
out" this first problem, even only theoretically, that the solutions to the
other ends will eventually present themselves to thought through new
possible intuitions and an awakened power to imagine a universal political constitution of the human race. Finally, it is only in the name of
this final end, the "political determination of the human species in the
last instance," that a rule could even appear as the first principle of any
future political philosophy, or what I have merely called "post-war philosophy," and for which this study serves only as a prolegomena to future
research.

Acknowledgments

This study of "conceptual personae" in contemporary political philosophy has evolved over the past fourteen years since the publication of *The Non-Philosophy of Gilles Deleuze* (2002). Several earlier versions of the following chapters have appeared in journals or edited collections, and I wish to thank the following editors: Ian Buchanan, Eduardo Cadava, Jodi Dean, Aaron Levy, Forbes Morlock, and Nick Thoburn.

This work represents a significant departure from my earlier method of "non-philosophical" commentary, primarily on the works of Gilles Deleuze and Jacques Derrida, and thus was made to serve as a theoretical accompaniment and prolegomena to the Perpetual Peace Project, a large-scale curatorial initiative that was copartnered since 2008 with Aaron Levy (Slought, Philadelphia), Martin Rauchbauer (Deutsche Haus, New York University), and Rosi Braidotti (Centre for the Humanities, Utrecht University). I would like to express my gratitude to all the contributors who were involved in different phases of this public project, who have all taught me the true meaning of creative collaboration. This book is dedicated to these "friends of peace."

I would also like to pay homage to the cities and the people of Amsterdam and Utrecht for providing the background, context, and, ironically, the birthplace and final destination of both projects.

I thank Neil West, Scott Mueller, Sheila McMahon, Erin Warholm-Wohlenhaus, Anne Wrenn, and Bresser-Chapple for all details of production and design. Finally, I express my sincere appreciation and gratitude to my editor at the University of Minnesota Press, Douglas Armato, who suffered through numerous conceptual versions of this project with both patience and perspective, until what first appeared as a "crazy etymological exercise" gradually resembled a new vocabulary of political concepts and terms, even if they still belong to a foreign language. As Jorge Luis Borges once said of the "good reader," these days a "good editor" is an even more rare and exotic bird and thus should be prized above all the other birds of knowledge in an author's personal aviary.

Notes

INTRODUCTION

1. Deleuze and Guattari, *What Is Philosophy?*, 329–30. This is a question of ontology that Deleuze and Guattari share with Derrida, who, in his treatise *The Politics of Friendship* published three years later in 1994, writes the following: "The question 'What is friendship?' but also 'Who is the friend (both or either sex)?' is nothing but the question: 'What is Philosophy?'" Derrida, *The Politics of Friendship*, 240.

2. This is a term Deleuze employs more frequently in his later writings and interviews to characterize the democratic ideal of friendship based on the values of consensus and "free" communication. As Deleuze asks, "*Peut-être la parole, la communication, sont-elles pourries?*" The French adjective *pourri* indicates a much stronger sense of something being rotten, the term "corrupted" being a figurative translation. Accordingly, one of the major arguments put forward in the conclusion of their last work is that the political idea of friendship—understood as the democratic consensus of friends or equals, as well as the instruments of speech and communication—has become corrupted by being completely permeated by money (for example, appearing today as the intersubjective idealism of globalized markets proposed by contemporary neoliberalists). See Deleuze, *Pourparlers*, 238; Deleuze and Guattari, *What Is Philosophy?*, 7ff.

3. Deleuze and Guattari, *What Is Philosophy?*, 18.

4. Ibid., 8.

5. Benveniste, *Le Vocabulaire*, 1:337–38.

6. Ibid., 1:338.

7. For another excellent commentary on Benveniste's etymology, see McNulty, *The Hostess*, viiiff.

8. Kant, *Perpetual Peace*, 118.

9. Deleuze and Guattari, *What Is Philosophy?*, 4.

10. Arendt, *The Origins of Totalitarianism*, 462.

11. Ibid.

12. For the quotation by Hayek, see Mirowski and Plehwe, *The Road from Mont Pelerin*, 435ff.

13. Mascolo, *Autour d'un effort de mémoire*, 65.

14. Deleuze, *Negotiations*, 174.

15. Deleuze and Guattari, *What Is Philosophy?*, 10.

16. Ibid., 3.

17. Ibid., 2.

18. I am referring not only to Heidegger's role in the National Socialist Party but also to the betrayal of the philosophical friendship with Edmund Husserl when he removed his previous dedication to his teacher in a later edition of *Zein und Zeit*. This act of betrayal was and remains, certainly, unforgiveable.

19. Deleuze and Guattari, *What Is Philosophy?*, 109.

20. Of course, here I am alluding also to Paul Celan's meditation on the Heideggerian figures of the poet and the thinker in "The Conversation in the Mountains." See Celan, *Collected Prose*, 17–22.

21. Deleuze and Guattari, *What Is Philosophy?*, 87ff. See also Gregory Flaxman's excellent discussion of Greek autochthony in *Gilles Deleuze*, 94ff.

22. Deleuze and Guattari, *What Is Philosophy?*, 68.

23. Benveniste, *Le Vocabulaire*, 1:360.

24. Agamben, *Homo Sacer*, 71, 149.

25. Of course, Agamben's conceptual persona of *homo sacer* is already in many respects, if not in most, completely indebted to the earlier testimonies of Primo Levi and Robert Antelme. First, we can point to Agamben's appropriation of the figure of the *Muselmann*, where we first find the definition of "bare life" as the place where *bios* is so concentrated in *zoē* as to become indistinguishable from it—literally, a "zone of indistinction" between political life and biological life. Secondly, in the introduction to *Homo Sacer*, there is indeed an oblique reference to the "testimony of Robert Antelme," which cites Antelme's major proclamation that the experience of the camps provokes an almost "biological assertion of the belonging together of the human species" (that is, of the certainty of the unity of man, and not his irremediable division, given that the SS were indeed men like us, and thus there can be no

alibi of difference that would only recapitulate, on a moral level, the fundamental assertion of every racist ideology). And yet, this claim is an example of a modern aporia, which is nothing less than the inner solidarity between modern democracy and totalitarianism, both of which make the quality of biopolitical life "the most supreme political principle" (10).

26. Although Deleuze ascribes the new conceptual persona of the philosopher, as a "Socrates who becomes Jewish," to the writings of Maurice Blanchot, certainly two other modern philosophers come to mind who are barely mentioned in Deleuze's writings: Levinas and Derrida. Of course, this is not simply an oversight, but the reasons for this neglect bear a complex personal history.

27. For a characterization of Antelme's own speech, see the foreword to *The Human Race*, 3–5.

28. For example, see recent essays by Agamben and Braidotti in Wilmer and Žukauskaitė, *Resisting Biopolitics*, 21ff.

29. This is one of the questions raised by a collective research group that Cary Wolfe and I cofounded in 2013, The Society for the Study of Biopolitical Futures. See http://biopoliticalfutures.net.

30. Deleuze and Guattari, *What Is Philosophy?*, 31.

31. Ibid.

32. Certainly two thinkers that come immediately to mind to demonstrate this nonphilosophical understanding are Schmitt and Marx, both of whom I discuss below around the conceptual persona of the "enemy."

33. Many of Kant's own contemporaries, including Johann Wolfgang von Goethe, took *Toward Perpetual Peace* to be Kant's attempt at being humorous, or merely ironic, and in the centuries that followed most philosophers did not take it seriously. Even today there are those who view the later writings as evidence of dementia and diminishing mental capacity, certainly compared with the period of the *Critique of Pure Reason*. Most recently, Kant's dementia has been the subject of psychiatric speculation, and one article provides a diagnosis of *dementia praecox* (an earlier term for schizophrenia), which was organically the result of a tumor in the frontal lobe. See Marchand, "Emmunuel Kant's Dementia," 35–39.

34. Deleuze and Guattari, *What Is Philosophy?*, 107.

35. Ibid.

36. Of course, "the shame of being human" is a major theme first announced by Primo Levi, which is frequently referenced by Deleuze, as well as by Blanchot and Derrida.

37. Benveniste, *Le Vocabulaire*, 1:337.

38. Arendt, *The Origins of Totalitarianism*, 462.

39. Ibid.

40. Derrida, *Rogues*, 100ff.

41. Kant, *Perpetual Peace*, 117.

42. This has served as the basic principle of the Perpetual Peace Project and the large-scale curatorial initiative that I cofounded in 2008 with Aaron Levy (Slought, Philadelphia) and Martin Rauchbauer (Deutsche Haus, New York University) and that, in 2012, sponsored exhibitions and events at Utrecht University in commemoration of the three hundredth anniversary of the Treaty of Utrecht (i.e., The Peace of Utrecht). See www.redraftingperpetual peace.org.

43. Deleuze and Guattari, *A Thousand Plateaus*, 422.

44. Kant, *Metaphysical Elements of Justice*, 29.

1. FRIEND (FR. *L'AMI*)

1. Deleuze, *Two Regimes of Madness*, 329–30.

2. Cicero, *Old Age, Friendship, and Divination*, 55–56.

3. Here I am particularly thinking of Beckett's later play "Catastrophe," which portrays three "talking heads" in overlapping monologue about themselves and their relationships.

4. I continue to employ the French term in parentheses to echo the Heideggerian term for existential care *(Sorge)*, which is *Angst*.

5. A good illustration of the kind of conversation I am referring to, in which the unspeakable constitutes the linguistic condition of enunciation, expressed in the forms of prattle and idle speech between friends, is Paul Celan's "Conversation in the Mountains," which also cryptically refers to a conversation that did not take place between Celan and Heidegger and concerns the philosopher's infamous "silence" concerning the extermination of the Jews. Thus, I would include this "conversation" in the genealogy of "the friend who must be suspected" but will return to this in another context. See Celan, *Collected Prose*, 17–22.

6. Deleuze and Guattari, *What Is Philosophy?*, 4.

7. See Deleuze's earliest description of the Greek dialectic of rivalry *(amphisbetesis)* in *Logique du sens*, 292ff.

8. Here I am thinking of Althusser's famous claim that "ideology has no history," but would qualify this claim by observing that for Althusser this history is actually found in the progression of philosophical systems that each express the current stage of capitalism, from a stage of primitive accumulation to the full realization of the economic principle in "its last instance." See Althusser, *For Marx*, 87–128.

9. Deleuze, *Two Regimes of Madness*, 331.

10. Ibid. The full quotation is as follows: "Without the spirit of friendship, [the thoughts that form in the exchange of words, by writing or in person. Without that,] we are, by our own hands, outside thought." However, the source of this quote remains a mystery, since I cannot find it in Hölderlin's hymns. Mascolo himself acknowledges that it comes from a translation of one of Hölderlin's poems, most likely "As When on a Holiday," that reportedly Blanchot had translated and then published anonymously in the journal *Comité* in October 1968, perhaps in commemoration of the events of May '68. Here again, in other words, we seem to have the implication of a "secret" communication of an idea of friendship between Blanchot and Mascolo, a secret that is also ascribed to Antelme, who is often represented as a kind of French Hölderlin (one who returns from his madness in Germany), which Mascolo refers to in the passage above as "*this communism in thought*" (ibid.).

11. Here we might recall that Nietzsche could undergo a diet of atheism only through a creative spirit of friendship, particularly his friendship with women (and with Lou Ardreas-Salomé, in particular), which is the subject of one of the concluding hymns in *The Gay Science*.

12. Derrida, *The Politics of Friendship*, 75ff.

13. Deleuze, *Two Regimes of Madness*, 330.

14. Schmitt, *The Concept of the Political*, 36.

15. Marx and Engels, *The Marx-Engels Reader*, 133.

16. In *Search for a Method*, Sartre uses this metaphor of the sulfuric acid bath negatively to criticize the idealism implicit in orthodox Marxism, where Marx and Engels reduce human beings to emanations of the historical process foretold (44). Here I am using this metaphor in order to underline the process of "purification," in an anthropological sense, that also belonged to Marx's earlier division of the classes as a species differentiation and the identification of a new species *(Geschlecht)* that will emerge at the end of the historical process. I return to take up this analysis in relation to the modern scientific racism of National Socialist ideology in the chapter on Antelme. At this point it should be clear to the reader that my discussion is guided as much by Derrida's reflections on the subject as Deleuze's, which are more elliptical in the last writings.

17. Marx and Engels, *The Marx-Engels Reader*, 505–6.

18. Ibid., 506.

2. ENEMY (GER. *DER FEIND*)

1. Derrida, *The Politics of Friendship*, 116.

2. See also Strauss, "Notes on Schmitt," 108–17.

3. Schmitt, *The Concept of the Political*, 46.

4. Kant, *Perpetual Peace*, 102ff.

5. For a discussion of the crucial importance of this political constitution in the urban centers of the early Roman Empire, see Meeks, *The Origins of Christian Morality*, 37–52. Although derived from the original Greek *politeia* (civil constitution), as distinct from the later Christian *ekklesia* (gathering, or "assembly"), the juridical meaning of *politeuma* seems adapted to the specifically urban and colonial context of the Roman period, often referring to the political identity of groups of immigrant and resident aliens in Hellenic cities under Roman rule. The term even gains a further figurative sense after the second century, referring to the political constitution of Christians on earth: "Our home is in heaven, and here on earth we are a colony *[politeuma]* of heavenly citizens" (Bauer, *A Greek-English Lexicon*, 686).

6. In fact, only the Pauline gospel of Luke recounts a third trial of Jesus before Herod, reporting that once Pilate hears that Jesus is originally from Galilee, and therefore under Herod's "jurisdiction" *(ethousia)*, he remands the case to come before Herod in the sense of referring it back to a lower court. What is interesting in this context is that the gospel states that after this gesture Pilate and Herod become "friends," whereas they were "at enmity" beforehand (Luke 23:12). A further motive for Pilate's political strategizing is given by Flavius Josephus, who recounts that Pilate was already facing the revolt of the Jewish people against him for being the first Roman procurator to bring effigies of Caesar into Jerusalem in violation of Jewish law. This action resulted in a six-day petition by multitudes from the city, ending on the seventh with Pilate surrounding the crowds with soldiers and threatening to put them to death. As Josephus recounts this scene, the people threw themselves on the ground and bared their throats, "saying that they would take their deaths willingly rather than allowing the wisdom of their laws to be transgressed" (*The Complete Works*, 379), at which point Pilate relented and commanded that the images be withdrawn to Caesarea. I give here a more detailed account of this incident since Josephus provides it as a much better context for understanding Pilate's decision concerning Jesus, which Josephus refers to as one of the many "sad calamities" that put the Jews in disorder during Pilate's unhappy colonial administration as the Roman procurator of Judea. See Josephus, *The Antiquities of the Jews*, 379–80.

7. Schmitt, *The Concept of the Political*, 46.

8. Ibid., 28–29.

9. Conrad, *Heart of Darkness*, 62.

10. Quoted in Derrida, *The Politics of Friendship*, 134n.

11. Ibid., 116.

12. Schmitt, *The Concept of the Political*, 29.

13. Derrida, *The Politics of Friendship*, 114.

14. Ibid.

15. Derrida, *Of Hospitality*, 25.

16. See Levinas, "The Asymmetry of the Interpersonal," 215–16.

17. Levinas, *De l'existence à l'existant*, 95.

18. Levinas, *Totality and Infinity*, 254ff.

19. Leibniz, *The Shorter Leibniz Texts*, 97.

20. Cicero, *On Old Age, Friendship, and Divination*, 62.

21. Sartre, *Being and Nothingness*, 303.

3. FOREIGNER (LAT. *PERIGRINUS*)

1. Benveniste, *Le Vocabulaire*, 2:360.

2. Derrida, *Aporias*, 42ff. Of course, another way to address this structure would be to say that it is "purely historical," but then this only displaces and repeats the figure of aporia in another location, which now appears in the form of an absent mediator between nature and culture.

3. Simmel, *The Sociology of Georg Simmel*, 403. In his examples, Simmel often designates the relationship between the stranger and property by using two German words for "alienation" and "to alienate": *Entfremden*, which designates the affective and psychological sense of alienation; and *entäussern*, which designates the legal–commercial sense of alienation in the selling of property, the transference of ownership, and "making things external to oneself." This distinction within the concept of alienation itself bears an interesting determination of the stranger as an autotelic designation, since, as Simmel notes above, all strangers are "traders," implying that the activity of exchange is itself the result of the fact that the stranger is "no owner of the soil."

4. Derrida, *Of Hospitality*, 55.

5. Kant, *Perpetual Peace*, 103.

6. Kant, *Kant's Principles of Politics*, 101.

7. Kant, *Perpetual Peace*, 102.

8. Ibid.

9. Derrida, *Of Hospitality*, 55.

10. Heidegger, *Introduction to Metaphysics*, 128.

11. Kant, *Perpetual Peace*, 103.

12. Levinas, *De l'existence à l'existant*, xx.

13. Derrida, *De l'hospitalité*, 142.

14. For example, Simmel defines the psychological character of ambivalence (a feeling of "coolness" and perception of "detachment") that determines the relationship with a stranger. Because of this contradictory mixture of coolness in warmth and distance in nearness, Simmel's reading seems to prepare the possibility for the sudden turnabout and psychological repulsion against the stranger, which of course can also be inferred from the history of the European Jews. On the subjective qualities attached to social relations with strangers, see especially "The Stranger in Metropolitan Life," 405ff.

15. Derrida, *Of Hospitality*, 29.

16. Derrida, *De l'hospitalité*, 126.

17. Kant, *Perpetual Peace*, 103.

18. Ibid.

19. Ibid., 105.

4. STRANGER (GR. XÉNOS)

1. Benveniste, *Le Vocabulaire*, 1:337.

2. Ibid., 1:343.

3. Ibid.

4. Benveniste writes, "The verb phileîn (φιλεῖν), which does not only signify 'love,' or affection, but also, from the earliest texts onward, 'to kiss'; the derivative phílēma (φίλημα) signifies nothing else but 'kiss'" (ibid., 1:344).

5. Of course, Levinas draws on this archaic meaning in his argument concerning the original signification of the ethical relationship as "involuntary election." See Levinas, *Otherwise than Being*, 15.

6. Benveniste, *Le Vocabulaire*, 1:347.

7. Ibid.

8. Ibid., 1:344.

9. Ibid., 1:353 (my emphasis).

10. Ibid., 1:353.

11. Ibid., 1:338.

12. Ibid., 1:340.

13. Ibid., 1:341.

14. Ibid., 1:340.

15. Kant, *Kant's Principles of Politics*, 101.

16. Benveniste, *Le Vocabulaire*, 2:267.

5. DEPORTEE (FR. LE DÉPORTÉ)

1. Blanchot, *The Infinite Conversation*, 130ff.

2. Ibid.

3. Deleuze, *Two Regimes of Madness*, 330.

4. Antelme, "Man as the Basis of Right," 29.

5. Benslama, "Man's Property/Propriety," 71–82.

6. Antelme, "Poor Man—Proletarian—Deportee," 18.

7. Ibid. (my emphasis, first sentence).

8. Ibid., 19.

9. Ibid., 20.

10. Ibid., 21.

11. Ibid., 20.

12. Ibid., 21.

13. Ibid.

14. Ibid.

15. Ibid., 22.

16. Ibid.

17. Ibid., 22.

18. Mascolo, *Autour d'un effort de mémoire*, 23–24.

19. Blanchot, *The Infinite Conversation*, 135.

20. Mascolo, *Autour d'un effort de mémoire*, 88.

21. Antelme, *The Human Race*, 219.

22. Mascolo, *Autour d'un effort de mémoire*, 65.

23. Deleuze and Guattari, *A Thousand Plateaus*, 356.

24. Homer, quoted in Benveniste, *Le Vocabulaire*, 1:343–44.

25. These statements concerning the coming demographic disproportion between the richest and poorest populations globally deliberately echo a harrowing question posed by Derrida as early as 1994: "Does not the globalization of demographic reality and calculation render the probability of such a 'context' weaker than ever and as threatening for survival as the worst, the radical evil of the 'final solution'?" Derrida, *Acts of Religion*, 91.

6. A REVOLUTIONARY PEOPLE (FR. *LA MACHINE DE GUERRE*)

1. Plato, *Republic*, bk. 5, chapter 15.

2. Deleuze and Guattari, *A Thousand Plateaus*, 352.

3. Ibid.

4. Deleuze, *Essays Critical and Clinical*, 79.

5. This recalls the phrase used by Georges Bataille. See "Sacrificial Mutilation," 61–72.

6. Deleuze and Guattari, *A Thousand Plateaus*, 471.

7. Ibid., 423.

8. Ibid., 352, 419.

9. In this regard, Don Delillo's novel *The Names* is essentially a meditation on the problem of the molecular-becoming of a people, particularly with respect to the "exceptional individual" of the serial killer as a collective or group phenomenon that is more particular to democratic societies and, in the case of the novel, to the United States. See Delillo, *The Names*.

10. Arendt, *The Origins of Totalitarianism*, 477.

11. I am referring, of course, to the statement "Is it Useless to Revolt?" that appeared in *Le Monde* in 1979.

12. Foucault, *Power*, 450.

13. Ibid.

14. Adorno and Horkheimer, *Toward a New Manifesto*, 49.

15. Foucault, *Power*, 452.

16. Deleuze, *Deux régimes de fous*, 223. (I have used the original French version of this text [my translation].)

17. This statement was omitted from the English translation of *Two Regimes of Madness* (2007). See Stivale, review of *Two Regimes of Madness*, 82–92, for a detailed commentary.

18. Deleuze was also writing a year after the first major campaign of the Israel Defense Forces (IDF) in Beirut to uproot the Palestinian Liberation Organization (PLO), and five years before the first Intifada ("revolt").

19. Deleuze, *Deux régimes de fous*, 223.

20. Deleuze and Guattari, *A Thousand Plateaus*, 354.

21. Deleuze, *Essays Critical and Clinical*, 79.

22. Ibid. (my emphasis).

23. Deleuze and Guattari, *A Thousand Plateaus*, 355.

24. Ibid., 422.

25. Ibid., 356.

26. Ibid., 422.

27. Ibid., 426. In many regards, I find these questions have a profound resonance with the meditation at the heart of Terrence Mallick's *The Thin Red Line* (or the meditation on war in nature), where the main protagonist asks: "Who first started this war in nature?" "Who's killing us?"

28. Deleuze and Guattari, *A Thousand Plateaus*, 422.

29. Ibid., 425.

30. Derrida, *The Politics of Friendship*, 85.

31. Derrida, *Rogues*, 116.

32. Deleuze and Guattari, *A Thousand Plateaus*, 422.

33. Ibid., 423.

34. Ibid.

35. Deleuze, *Essays Critical and Clinical,* 79.

36. Deleuze and Guattari, *A Thousand Plateaus,* 422.

37. Ibid., 421–22.

38. Ibid., 421.

39. Deleuze, *Two Regimes of Madness,* 387. For the original story by Dickens, "A Respected Friend in a New Aspect," see *Our Mutual Friend,* 428–37.

CONCLUSION

1. Kant, *Kant's Principles of Politics,* 23.

2. Derrida also draws on Benveniste's rich analysis of the sovereignty of the master and the self in the seminar "The Beast and the Sovereign." See Derrida, *The Beast and the Sovereign,* 66ff.

3. Kant, *Kant's Principles of Politics,* 23.

4. In *The Beast and the Sovereign,* Derrida writes: "In other words, he is zoo-political, that's his essential definition, that's what is proper to him, *idion*; what is proper to man is politics; what is proper to this living being that man is, is politics, and therefore man is immediately zoo-political, in his very life, and the distinction between bio-politics and zoo-politics doesn't work at all here—moreover, neither Heidegger nor Foucault stays with this distinction, and it's obvious that already in Aristotle there's thinking of what is today called 'zoo-politics' or 'bio-politics'" (348–49). Here I cannot analyze this rich passage in detail, with its play on the senses of "peculiarity" in the Greek *idion* and the German *Eigentuemlich,* which is also made explicitly in reference to Heidegger's concept of *dasein.* Therefore, one might translate the above into the following proposition: *The one thing that is peculiar to human* dasein *is politics.*

5. Kant, *Kant's Principles of Politics,* 36–37 (my emphasis).

6. Ibid., 28.

7. Ibid., 30.

8. "This power as a cause working by laws which are unknown to us, is commonly called *Fate;* but in view of the design manifested in the course of the world, it is to be regarded as the deep wisdom of a Higher Cause directed towards the realization of the final purpose of the human race, and predetermining the course of the world by relation to it, and as such we call it *Providence*" (ibid., 62).

9. See Kant, *Perpetual Peace,* 118ff.

10. Antelme, "Poor Man—Proletarian—Deportee," 22.

11. Antelme, *The Human Race,* 219.

12. Ibid.

13. Ibid.

14. Kant, *Kant's Principles of Politics*, 27–28.

15. Foucault, *The Birth of Biopolitics*, 249ff.

16. Agamben, *Homo Sacer*, 11.

17. Derrida, *The Beast and the Sovereign*, 70–71.

18. Kant, *Kant's Principles of Politics*, 27.

19. This line occurs in the "Reflections on the Observations of the Beautiful and the Sublime," immediately after Kant also acknowledges that he has come to understand "his own deceptive feeling of superiority" with regard to the ordinary person, who was also capable of experiencing the same sublime sentiment of freedom as he was. See the *Critique of Pure Judgment*, AA 20.

20. Homer, quoted in Benveniste, *Le Vocabulaire*, 1:343–44.

21. Derrida and Vattimo, *Religion*, 72.

22. Derrida, *The Beast and the Sovereign*, 71.

23. Schmitt, *Die Verfassung der Freiheit*, quoted in Bendersky, *Carl Schmitt*, 229. At the same time, Bendersky argues that many of Schmitt's views during the years of 1935 and 1936, in particular, are motivated by his own political problems with the Nazi Party, especially the SS, who threatened to ostracize him for not being radical enough in his jurisprudence. Thus, like Heidegger during exactly the same period, Schmitt put on the wolf's uniform in order advance his career—or, at least, to protect it from serious harm. Also, both were motivated by the incredible arrogance and personal ambition that went along with being leading German academics. So that we don't immediately assume a tone of moral superiority, I imagine that if our colleagues in the academy today were put to the same test of character, we would discover that many of them might also prefer to be dressed up as wolves rather than appearing as sheep. As for myself, I would only hope I had the courage to choose poverty and ignominy over ambition—but one cannot be certain of such decisions.

24. Kant, *The Critique of Pure Reason*, A686/B714.

25. Kant, *Metaphysical Elements of Justice*, 159.

26. Kant, *Perpetual Peace*, 100.

27. Ibid., 107.

28. Quoted in Ellis, *Kant's Politics*, 80. The treaty in question is the Treaty of Aix-la-Chapelle (1748), which concluded the Austrian War of Succession with a *status quo ante bellum*—that is to say, the restoration of prewar territories and the recognition of Prussia's conquest of Silesia. It became the object of scorn by the French, in particular, and is referred to in popular sayings as the *Bête comme la paix* and *La guerre pour le roi de Prusse*, a resentment that became one of the motives for the conquests of the Napoleonic Wars.

29. Kant, *Perpetual Peace*, 107.

30. Ibid., 124. For a critical gloss on Kant's translation of this maxim, see Ellis, *Provisional Politics*, 10ff.

31. Cavallar, *Imperfect Cosmopolis*, 70ff.

32. Kant, *Perpetual Peace*, 115.

33. Wiesel, *Messengers of God*, 31.

34. Mitchell, *The Book of Job*, 397–98.

35. Wiesel, *Messengers of God*, 32.

36. Cavallar, *Imperfect Cosmopolis*, 72.

37. Ibid.

38. Ibid., 107.

39. Kant, *Perpetual Peace*, 116.

40. Kant, *Metaphysical Elements of Justice*, 162–63.

41. Ibid., 161.

42. Ibid., 162.

43. Ibid. (my emphasis).

44. Deleuze and Guattari, *What Is Philosophy?*, 110.

Bibliography

Agamben, Giorgio. *Homo Sacer: Sovereign Power and Bare Life.* Trans. Daniel Heller-Roazen. Palo Alto: Stanford University Press, 1998.

Adorno, Theodore, and Max Horkheimer. *Toward a New Manifesto.* London: Verso, 2011.

Althusser, Louis. *For Marx.* Trans. Ben Brewster. London: Verso, 2005.

———. *Lenin and Philosophy and Other Essays.* New York: Monthly Review Press, 2001.

Antelme, Robert. *The Human Race.* Trans. Jeffrey Haight and Annie Mahler. Marlboro, Vt.: Marlboro Press, 1992.

———. "Man as the Basis of Right." In Dobbels, *On Robert Antelme's "The Human Race,"* 27–30.

———. "Poor Man—Proletarian—Deportee." In Dobbels, *On Robert Antelme's "The Human Race,"* 17–22.

Arendt, Hannah. *The Origins of Totalitarianism.* New York: Harcourt, Brace, 1973.

Bataille, Georges. "Sacrificial Mutilation." In *Visions of Excess,* 61–72.

———. *Visions of Excess: Selected Writings, 1927–1939.* Trans. Alan Stoekl. Minneapolis: University of Minnesota Press, 1985.

Bauer, Walter. *A Greek-English Lexicon of the New Testament and Other Early Christian Literature.* Chicago: University of Chicago Press, 1957.

Beckett, Samuel. *The Collected Shorter Plays.* Vol. 3. New York: Grove Press, 1984.

Bendersky, Joseph J. *Carl Schmitt: Theorist for the Reich.* Princeton, N.J.: Princeton University Press, 2014.

Benslama, Fethi. "Man's Property/Propriety." In Dobbels, *On Robert Antelme's "The Human Race,"* 71–82.

Bentham, Jeremy. "A Plan for an Universal and Perpetual Peace." In *The Works of Jeremy Bentham*. Vol. 2. Ed. John Bowring. Edinburgh: William Tait, 1843.

Benveniste, Émile. *Le Vocabulaire des institutions Indo-Européennes*. Vol. 1. Paris: Minuit, 1966.

———. *Le Vocabulaire des institutions Indo-Européennes*. Vol. 2. Paris: Minuit, 1974.

Blanchot, Maurice. *The Infinite Conversation*. Trans. Susan Hanson. Minneapolis: University of Minnesota Press, 1993.

Cavallar, Georg. *Imperfect Cosmopolis: Studies in the History of International Legal Theory and Cosmopolitan Ideas*. Cardiff: University of Wales, 2011.

Celan, Paul. *Collected Prose*. Trans. Rosemary Waldrop. London: Carcanet Press, 1986.

Cicero. *On Old Age, Friendship, and Divination*. Cambridge, Mass.: Harvard University Press, 1923.

Conrad, Joseph. *The Heart of Darkness*. London: Penguin, 1995.

Deleuze, Gilles. *Deux régimes de fous: Textes et entretiens, 1975–1995*. Ed. David Lapoujade. Paris: Minuit, 2003.

———. *Essays Critical and Clinical*. Trans. Daniel W. Smith and Michael A. Greco. Minneapolis: University of Minnesota Press, 1997.

———. *Logique du sens*. Paris: Minuit, 1969.

———. *Negotiations*. Trans. Martin Joughin. New York: Columbia University Press, 1995.

———. *Pourparlers, 1972–1990*. Paris: Minuit, 1990.

———. *Two Regimes of Madness*. Trans. Amie Hodges and Mike Taormina. Cambridge, Mass.: MIT Press, 2005.

Deleuze, Gilles, and Félix Guattari. *A Thousand Plateaus*. Trans. Brian Massumi. Minneapolis: University of Minnesota Press, 1987.

———. "Treatise on Nomadology." In *A Thousand Plateaus,* 387–467.

———. *What Is Philosophy?* Trans. Hugh Tomlinson and Graham Burchell. New York: Columbia University Press, 1994.

Delillo, Don. *The Names*. New York: Vintage Books, 1989.

Derrida, Jacques. *Acts of Religion*. Ed. Gil Anidjar. New York: Routledge, 2002.

———. *Aporias: Dying—Awaiting (One Another at) the "Limits of Truth" (Mourir—s'attendre Aux "limites de la Vérité")*. Palo Alto: Stanford University Press, 1993.

———. *The Beast and the Sovereign*. Vol. 1. Trans. Geoffrey Bennington. Chicago: University of Chicago Press, 2009.

———. *De l'hospitalité*. Paris: Calmann- Lévy, 1997.

———. *Of Hospitality.* Trans. Rachel Bowlby. Palo Alto: Stanford University Press, 2000.

———. *The Politics of Friendship.* Trans. George Collins. London: Verso Press, 1997.

———. *Rogues: Two Essays on Reason.* Trans. Pascale-Anne Brault and Michael Naas. Palo Alto: Stanford University Press, 2005.

Derrida, Jacques, and Gianni Vattimo. *Religion.* Palo Alto: Stanford University Press, 1998.

Dickens, Charles. *Our Mutual Friend.* London: Penguin Books, 1997.

Dobbels, Daniel, ed. *On Robert Antelme's "The Human Race."* Evanston, Ill.: Marlboro Press/Northwestern University Press, 2003.

Ellis, Elizabeth. *Kant's Politics: Provisional Theory for an Uncertain World.* New Haven: Yale University Press, 2005.

———. *Provisional Politics: Kantian Arguments in Policy Context.* New Haven: Yale University Press, 2014.

Flaxman, Gregory. *Gilles Deleuze and the Fabulation of Philosophy.* Minneapolis: University of Minnesota Press, 2012.

Foucault, Michel. *The Birth of Biopolitics.* Trans. Graham Burchell. New York: Palgrave Macmillan, 2008.

———. *Power. Essential Works of Foucault.* Vol. 3. Ed. James D. Faubion. New York: New Press, 1994.

Heidegger, Martin. *Erläuterungen zu Holderlin's Dichtung.* Frankfurt-am-Main: Klostermann, 1951.

———. *Introduction to Metaphysics.* New Haven: Yale University Press, 2000.

Josephus, Flavius. *The Antiquities of the Jews.* In *The Complete Works,* 379–80.

———. *The Complete Works.* Trans. William Whiston. Grand Rapids, Mich.: Kregel, 1960.

Kant, Immanuel. *Critique of Pure Judgment.* Vol. 11. Acadamische Ausgabe. Berlin: de Gruyter, 1968.

———. *Critique of Pure Reason.* Vol. 8. Acadamische Ausgabe. Berlin: de Gruyter, 1968.

———. *Kant's Principles of Politics: Including His Essay on Perpetual Peace. A Contribution to Political Science.* Ed. William Hastie. Edinburgh: T. & T. Clark, 1891.

———. *Metaphysical Elements of Justice.* 2nd ed. Trans. John Ladd. Indianapolis: Hackett, 1999.

———. *Perpetual Peace and Other Essays.* Trans. Ted Humphrey. Indianapolis: Hackett, 1983.

Kautila. *Arthashastra.* Bk. VI, *The Source of Sovereign States.* Translated by R. Shamasastry. Bangalore: Government Press, 1915.

Leibniz, Gottfried W. *The Shorter Leibniz Texts.* Ed. Lloyd Strickland. London: Continuum Books, 2006.

Levinas, Emmanuel. "The Asymmetry of the Interpersonal." In *Totality and Infinity,* 215–16.

———. *De l'existence à l'existant.* Paris: Fontaine, 1947.

———. *Otherwise than Being or Beyond Essence.* The Hague: Martinus Nijhoff, 1981.

———. *Totality and Infinity: An Essay on Exteriority.* Trans. Alphonse Lingis. Pittsburgh: Duquesne University Press, 1969.

Marchand, J. C. "Was Emmunuel Kant's Dementia Symptomatic of a Frontal Tumor?" *Revue Neurol* 153, no. 1 (1997): 35–39.

Marx, Karl, and Fredrick Engels. *The Marx-Engels Reader.* Ed. Robert C. Tucker. New York: W. W. Norton, 1978.

Mascolo, Dionys. *Autour d'un effort de mémoire: Sur une letter de Robert Antelme.* Paris: Maurice Nadeau, 1987.

McNulty, Tracy. *The Hostess: Hospitality, Femininity, and the Expropriation of Identity.* Minneapolis: University of Minnesota Press, 2007.

Meeks, Wayne A. *The Origins of Christian Morality: The First Two Centuries.* New Haven: Yale University Press, 1993.

Mirowski, Philip, and Dieter Plehwe, eds. *The Road from Mont Pelerin: The Making of a Neoliberal Thought Collective.* Cambridge, Mass.: Harvard University Press, 2009.

Mitchell, Stephen. *The Book of Job.* New York: HarperCollins, 2009. Kindle edition.

Sartre, Jean-Paul. *Being and Nothingness.* Trans. Hazel E. Barnes. New York: Philosophical Library, 1956.

———. *Search for a Method.* New York: Vintage Books, 1968.

Schmitt, Carl. *The Concept of the Political.* Chicago: University of Chicago Press, 1996.

Simmel, Georg. *The Sociology of Georg Simmel.* Ed. Kurt H. Wolff. New York: Free Press, 1950.

———. "The Stranger in Metropolitan Life." In *The Sociology of Georg Simmel,* 402–8.

Stivale, Charles. Review of *Two Regimes of Madness. Deleuze Studies* 1, no. 1 (2007): 82–92.

Strauss, Leo. "Notes on Schmitt: *The Concept of the Political.*" In Schmitt, *The Concept of the Political,* 108–17.

Wiesel, Elie. *Messengers of God.* New York: Simon and Schuster, 1985.

Wilmer, S. E., and Audronė Žukauskaitė. *Resisting Biopolitics: Philosophical, Political, and Performative Strategies.* London: Routledge Press, 2016.

Index

species, 22, 140, 144; of man, 19;
of right, 146; of the world, 158
cosmopolitism: arguments, 154;
centers, 6; constitution, 142, 148;
Cosmo-political Right, 148;
design of Nature, 141; juridical,
155; weak, 152
critique, 40

Deleuze, Gilles, 1–3, 5, 7–9, 10–13,
15–16, 17, 19, 23–24, 27–28, 30–36,
38, 41–42, 59, 60, 62, 90, 99, 100,
115, 120–23, 126–34, 135, 158, 159,
163n1, 165n26
depolitization, 147
déporté, 98, 99
deportee, 10, 14–17, 45, 69, 78, 99,
100, 103, 105–7, 109, 110, 112, 113,
141, 152; enemy, 105
democracy, 20, 38, 40, 126, 144, 160,
165; to come, 18, 143. *See also*
absolute democracy; universal
democracy
Derrida, Jacques, 4, 9, 15, 18, 21, 23,
37, 45, 46, 55–59, 61, 66, 71, 73, 77,
80–81, 91, 93, 127, 132, 138, 140,
143, 145, 147, 154, 159, 165n26,
167n16, 171n25, 173n4; globalatinization, 147; manner of speaking, 29
determination, in the last instance,
141, 143, 160, 166n8. *See also*
nonphilosophy
deterritorialization, 12, 123; conceptual personae, 11; earth, 159; and
reterritorialization, 20. *See also*
reterritorialization; territory
Dickens, Charles, 135
differend, 31

doxa, 144–45, 159
dream-work, 4, 5, 66, 88, 97
Duldsamkeit. See tolerance
Duldung. See tolerance
Duras, Marguerite, 15, 17, 35
durcharbeiten, 2, 141

ego, 30, 35, 60–62, 75–76; recognition, 61; social, 76
ekklesia, 5, 168n5
enemy, 3, 8, 9, 11, 14, 15, 24, 32, 37,
39–41, 45–47, 52–61, 64, 70, 71, 72,
80, 94, 106, 108, 109, 112, 119, 120,
131–32, 134, 153, 159; deportee-
enemy, 105; distinction, 63;
opposition, 4; relationship, 46;
unspecified, 24, 134. *See also*
friend-enemy; stranger: enemy
Engels, Friedrich, 39, 41, 57, 167
enigma of revolts, 125, 131
ens creatum, 96
entäusern, 169n3
entfremden, 78, 169n3. *See also*
estrangement
Entity, 34–35
Entpolitisierung. See depolitization
eros, 60, 61
Esposito, Robert, 16
estrangement, 74, 78, 97. See also
entfremden
ethné, 12, 51
ethnocentrism, 61, 114
etymology, 3, 66, 90; analysis, 2, 4,
88; exercise, 3, 5, 162; fallacy, 5;
history, 3, 4; investigation, 90

fascism, 9, 124, 126; death, 115, 132,
134; postfascist figure, 134
Feind. See enemy

GREGG LAMBERT is Dean's Professor of Humanities in the College of Arts and Sciences, Syracuse University, New York. Between 2008 and 2014 he was founding director of the Syracuse University Humanities Center and is currently director of the Central New York Humanities Corridor. He is author of numerous books, most recently *Return Statements: The Return of Religion in Contemporary Philosophy* and *In Search of a New Image of Thought: Gilles Deleuze and Philosophical Expressionism* (Minnesota, 2012).